Inspiring Stories of Resilience

Inspiring Stories of Resilience

PHEBE TROTMAN
& Thriving Entrepreneurs

PUBLISHED BY PHEBE TROTMAN

Never Quit on a Bad Day™
Inspiring Stories of Resilience
Phebe Trotman & Thriving Entrepreneurs

Cover Design & Layout by Margaret Cogswell Designs

Ordering Information:
Special discounts are available on large quantity purchases.
For details: please contact hello@neverquitonabadday.com

To my mother, Joyce, and in memory of my father, Henderson, who always taught my brother TeRoi and me to dream big, set goals and take action. Thank you for always supporting and cheering us on as we pursue our dreams.

"Let your light shine before others, that they may see your good deeds and glorify your Father in heaven."
(Matthew 5:16)

and

To my nieces Skylar and Tatum, may you always dream big and confidently go after your dreams.

"'For I know the plans I have for you,' declares the Lord, 'plans to prosper you and not to harm you, plans to give you hope and a future.'"
(Jeremiah 29:11)

TABLE OF CONTENTS

FOREWORD

By Vanessa Hunter

Top 50 Women Leaders in San Diego,
Author, and Motivational Speaker

It's about time!!! As in everything Phebe Trotman does, she has poured her heart and soul into creating this book. I've known Phebe since 2013 and I've never seen her give half effort to anything. In fact, her athlete's heart and passion just come shining through in everything she does and this book is no exception. On her way to the top, she has had to overcome many setbacks in life – both on and off the soccer field, and yet she keeps on showing up. When many people would throw in the towel, Phebe doubles down and rises like a phoenix from the ashes... not to survive, but to thrive.

Where does that come from? Is it genetic? Nature or nurture?

We've all had those moments when we've reached a roadblock and we've thought; "This is it, I can't keep doing this any longer!" Whether you have experienced a learning disability like Jimmy will share with you, or had the entire opportunity pulled out from under you like Steve, or had to push the reset button multiple times, like Phebe did, you've all had that moment when life didn't seem fair and you wanted to quit—haven't you?

What fascinates me about the stories that Phebe has gathered on the following pages is the quality of tenacity the authors share. Which begs the question; What makes some people persevere through the most monumental adversity while others crumble and quit at the slightest challenge? Is it based on their personal circumstances or the values they were raised with? Is it their resilience or coping skills? Is it a personality trait or mindset? Is it a skill they've developed based on prior experiences? Or is it as simple as the optimists versus the pessimists—you know, those glass half full or half empty people?

I've always said; "The decisions you make today will limit or expand the choices you have in the future." Because of this core belief, I rarely make impulsive decisions. I am far more likely to be slow to make a decision because I'm weighing, not just the immediate decision, but the entire trajectory of this one decision! (Talk about pressure!) And yet—I too have faced times when I wanted to quit. Times when a job or a relationship or a project just wasn't heading in the right direction. Or other times when I was challenged mentally and physically to the point of utter tears and exhaustion and yes, I wanted to quit! So, what made me go on?

Well, you know what they say; when you are at your wits end—reach out to someone for support. Often people will turn to a close friend or family member. But what happens when you do that and you don't get what you are looking for at all. In fact, you get a smack down of epic proportions because you "don't have a real job." Then what do you do? And by that I mean, what did I do? I yelled and cried about how unfair life is and then I prayed for guidance and mercy. I felt so alone. And therein lies the most epic challenge in coping with adversity; feeling alone on the battlefield.

When we feel like we are the only ones going through the muck—it's very difficult to find the motivation to keep going and dig our way out. In fact, most often we don't even know which way to turn to start digging! It's an isolating and disorienting feeling that leaves us paralyzed with fear of making the wrong move. In other words, we feel so deep in the hole that our next move could just be the one that wrecks it all! We are afraid that everything we've worked so hard for, everything we have sacrificed for—is now just a dream of bygone days.

The simple truth is that people in network marketing are lured by the promise of setting their own hours, working with whomever they want and being their own boss, although most people have absolutely no experience with any of those things. Furthermore, most entrepreneurial opportunities don't come with a training manual or a set of standard operating procedures. So, unless you have an exceptionally systematized enroller, you are often on your own and bound to face obstacles along the way. And even if you are fortunate enough to have someone showing you the way, there will be bumps in the road that will make you want to quit—if only for a moment. It happens to the best of us.

Having faced my fair share of adversity AND having spent the better part of three decades in network marketing, I'm thrilled to introduce you to Phebe's collection of stories of people who have overcome incredible obstacles in this industry. Whether you are a network marketer, an entrepreneur, a parent or a student of life, you'll resonate with some of the stories and identify with the challenges, thoughts and feelings you share with each contributor. You'll recognize qualities and core values within them.

The reality of this life is that you are NEVER totally alone. The simple knowledge that we have ALL faced and overcome "something" is exactly the wisdom we need so that we don't feel alone in the wake of adversity. In fact, that's what this book is all about. Phebe has brilliantly compiled stories from people who have taken chances that sometimes didn't pay off. People who weren't treated fairly. People who wanted to create a life of their dreams and got gut-punched. People who experienced disappointment, and many, many more. In other words, these stories are from people just like you!

As if creating the perfect recipe for your success, Phebe offers you strength and camaraderie within these pages. Among the stories and her enlightening end of chapter reflections, you'll find tips and strategies for cultivating resilience and perseverance in your own life. Hopefully, these stories will inspire and motivate you to keep going when the going gets tough. And in the end you'll know why you'll **Never Quit On a Bad Day!**

MY INSPIRATION

The Purpose Behind the Pages

MY INSPIRATION
The Purpose Behind the Pages

The idea for this book came to me on a late fall evening while visiting two dear friends in their gorgeous, custom designed home overlooking the beautiful Pacific Ocean. We chatted about a lot of topics, including our childhood to present day and, as entrepreneurs often do when getting together, we talked a lot about our businesses and journey as business owners.

Being in business definitely has provided some incredible highs, but there have also been some lows, too. My friends have created tremendous success with their online business and I have reached the top rank with my network marketing company. But believe me when I say it hasn't been without its challenges—and there have been a lot.

We talked about the good, the bad and the ugly in the life of an entrepreneur. We all agreed that if more people saw more of the good, they may persevere through the bad and the ugly. We joked about how it would be a really fun documentary for people to watch and really see what happens "behind the curtains."

We started talking about "what's next" for all of us. I shared that for the last several years, it has been on my heart to create something to help encourage people. I've been inspired by so many others over my life and they suggested that I write a book. I smiled and laughed at the idea because it wasn't the first time people have suggested I write a book and I always have had a list of "reasons," and doubts.

Have you ever had one of those moments where you know you should do something but doubt starts to take over? Yes, this still happens to me, too. Thankfully, over the years, I have learned to embrace that uncomfortable feeling. As an athlete and entrepreneur, I have started getting very good at getting comfortable with being uncomfortable. One of my favorite quotes is, "Life begins at the edge of your comfort zone" - Neale Donald Walsch (another highly recommended saying to remember and words to live by). Now, although I recognized that "feeling of discomfort," it doesn't mean I had fully embraced the idea of writing a book, because I still hadn't.

15

However, earlier that evening, when we were sharing about our journeys in our businesses. I had shared with them that one of my main motivations for hitting the top rank in my company is that I wanted other people to see that someone like them could do it. No matter your ethnicity, culture, age, background or qualifications, you can still do it. All you have to do is keep pushing through the tough days! As I was telling my friends my reasons (basically excuses) why I didn't want to write a book. They reminded me that a book isn't for me, it's for the readers that the book can touch and inspire. Which was the same reason why I worked so hard alongside an amazing team of rockstars to hit my company's top rank.

I still wasn't convinced, as I knew if I was going to write a book, I had to believe that the content of the book would be of value to the readers. I had to be inspired by the theme for the book and the book had to help other people.

Recently, I had the privilege of being inducted into the Coquitlam Sports Hall of Fame for my athletic success as a soccer player. During an interview, I was asked, "What does soccer mean to you, and what has it given you?" Soccer and sports in general have given me so much over the years—teamwork, discipline, accountability, confidence, leadership, perseverance, determination, resilience, time-management, patience, respect, emotional intelligence, lifelong friendships and so much more. I shared with the interviewer that so many life skills I've learned through playing the game of soccer, have actually come from many of the challenges that I have experienced over the years playing in sports. I shared that we highlight and celebrate the National Championships, the Gold Medals, the Player of the Year and MVP awards. However, it really is experiencing the heartbreaking losses, the silver and bronze medals (or no medals at all), not making the starting lineup, not playing in a game, being cut from a team, being sidelined with injuries, the extra skills and training times and even when frustrated, continuing to play is why and how I was able to enjoy the successes in sports too.

When chatting with my friends about writing a book, I remembered what I shared at the Coquitlam Sports Hall of Fame induction event and it all came together.

I believe that in business, in sports, in relationships, and in life, we need to share more of the tough stuff. We need to share about the challenging days. In business, we need to share more about the days when we don't want to make another phone call or host/attend a meeting, the days when everyone says "no," the days when a leader on your team leaves, the days the compensation plan gets changed. In sports, we need to share about the days we get cut from a team, the days we don't want to do the extra training, the days we don't want to work out, and the days we want to quit! We need to start sharing about the challenging moments and frustrating days when we ask ourselves, "Is it even worth it?" More importantly, we need to share what we did (or didn't do) to push through those days. We know all people have tough days but really, how hard are those days and what, how, why did they keep going.

This book is filled with a few of these stories— stories from people I look up to and who have inspired me along my journey. It is filled with their stories about a challenging time and why they didn't quit. What I'm most excited for you to read and learn is what they did or even didn't do to push through to keep going. You'll hear from them the emotions that they felt, the thoughts they had, and what happened during that time. It's wonderful to hear the exciting achievements and awards that others have accomplished and see the highlight reel of the VIP lifestyle they've been able to create as business owners, but I believe it's in those challenging moments and bad days that we really grow into the person and leader we are meant to be. Your bad moments and day(s) will most likely look a little different than the stories you will read in this book and other books in this series, but there will be parallels. Also, at the end of every chapter, you'll find a section titled Reflections on Resilience. This segment features a series of reflective questions designed to guide you on your personal growth journey. These exercises will prompt you to reflect on your own experiences and also provide practical tips and encouragement to help you reach your goals. My prayer is that you will connect with a moment or a tip in one of these stories and in the reflection exercises that will help you find, remember, grow in your resilience and strength so together, we can inspire our friends, our family, our teams, our communities to **Never Quit on a Bad Day!**

CHAPTER 1

THE SKY'S THE LIMIT

Jordan Adler

THE SKY'S THE LIMIT

Jordan Adler

I was an entrepreneur from a young age, growing up in the south suburbs of Chicago. I was always looking for ways to make money. At the age of seven, I put on puppet and ventriloquist shows, and charged a quarter for friends to attend my shows. I also had a neighborhood weekly newspaper route where my payment was tips, and I made sure to deliver on time every week, whether there was a snowstorm or if it was a scorching hot day. I wasn't competitive (and still am not), but I am creative and resourceful, and try to give people what they're looking for. I've found people will redo their priorities if you give them something that they just can't live without.

One of my most challenging days came quite a few years later, when I was 47. I live in Las Vegas and my condo on the 24th floor of the Waldorf on the Vegas Strip has a front-row view of tour helicopters that take passengers on trips to experience the Vegas lights from the sky.

I wondered what it would be like to be the pilot, and give my own friends rides in my helicopter to see Las Vegas from the air. And where else could I go if I had my helicopter pilot license? The next morning, I went online and searched for "helicopter pilot lessons." It brought back a result for 702 Helicopters, a company in North Las Vegas. I booked a Discovery Flight where, for $250, I would get to go up with an instructor and learn what it would take to get my license. Brian Lorenz gave me a tour of the facility and then of the helicopter itself and how it works.

And then we went for a flight, where I was introduced to the gauges and controls. He even let me take control and fly for a few minutes! Well, I caught the bug and plopped down $30,000 to get my license. Little did I know that it was going to eventually cost me $100,000, and this experience was going to be one of the hardest things I had ever taken on in my life!

It's all fun until you have to learn to do things that are scary and difficult. Looking back on the experience now, there were probably more than 100 times when

I wanted to quit. **When you want to quit something, I've found you start lying to yourself and even make up legitimate reasons why you can't continue.**

Hovering (holding the helicopter steady about four to five feet off the ground) took hours to learn. Each time I would go to learn how to hover the helicopter, I would ask my instructor Travis, "Have you ever had someone come through who couldn't do it?" I was concerned that it was beyond my skill to learn how to hover. It was very difficult and took many hours to get just this one skill dialed in. At one point, Travis said, "If you can keep it within a football field, I'll buy you a pizza!" And if it wasn't for him saving my ass over and over again, I wouldn't be here to tell the story!

Also, hovering is just one of about 40 skills you are required to master before you can get your helicopter pilot license. It's honestly quite overwhelming, especially since many of the things you need to do have to be done simultaneously.

One skill you must master is autorotation—a simulation of engine failure. The maneuver is done by rolling off the throttle and lowering the collective, which disconnects the drive train (engine) from the main rotor. You must learn how to "glide" the helicopter down to safety without an engine. You must immediately lower the collective, stabilize the descent, assess wind, quickly pick a place to land, turn the helicopter into the wind, establish a glide speed and rate of descent, etc. Lots to do, all at once. And you need to do this over 150 times until you master it—fortunately, with the help of your instructor. Still, it's quite scary for the first 100 times.

For most normal people (granted, getting a helicopter pilot license is probably not normal) fear can easily shut you down and cause you to quit. There were so many times that I wanted to throw in the towel because I wasn't sure if I was up to the challenge, and it's the setbacks that can cause you to quit. It's so easy to give up—but you'll never have your dream if you quit. And my dream of flying was bigger and more important than my fears, so I forced myself to go in over and over again. Just keep putting one foot in front of the other.

I adopted the mantra, "See the job through, no matter what." And after two years of training and practice testing, I was awarded my private helicopter pilot license and now have over 300 hours of flying. One of my favorite things to do is to take friends over the Spring Mountain Preserve to the Pahrump Winery for lunch. The flight is stunningly beautiful. The whole trip, including lunch, takes about four hours. It's a perfect way to spend an afternoon.

My dream faced another unexpected challenge after many, many flights. I decided I wanted my own helicopter, so I hired a broker and spent months traveling the country to find the right one. When I finally found it, I purchased the helicopter and I had it shipped to Vegas from the swamps of Louisiana. After reassembly and inspections and lots and lots of out of state training, I got to solo in it for the first time. What a dream!

I had a close friend introduce me to a guy that said he had a hangar facility with many helicopters and thousands of hours flying. We spent lots of time together over a period of months and one day I invited him to join me in my helicopter for a short flight. While we were hovering, I asked him if he wanted to take the controls and he said yes. He took the controls and within a quarter of a second, the helicopter was spinning out of control. We crashed into a 150-gallon fuel tank.

The next thing I know, I remember hearing people screaming, "Get the &%$ out!" as fuel rained down on us, and they feared an explosion was imminent. In that moment, I felt a gripping fear was anchored into my very being.

After the crash, I felt defeated in so many ways. Will I ever fly again? Why did this happen to me? Am I really supposed to be flying? And to make matters worse, after the NTSB and FAA conducted their investigations, it was determined that the guy I was flying with had never flown a helicopter in his life! He was a scam artist and had convinced me and everyone in his life that he was an experienced commercial helicopter pilot!

And even though the crash was not my fault, I had gripping fear and some PTSD about getting back up in the air. I found myself continually re-running the movie of the crash in my mind. It haunted me. I could hear the sound of the thrashing metal and breaking glass and I could smell the fuel raining down on me. After months of repeating the crash over and over again in my mind, I found that the fear and not my dream was controlling me.

I was reminded (as I had been in the past) that the key to breaking through any obstacle is to first refocus on your dream, then release the past, and finally, take action—regardless of anything else. I needed to follow my own advice if I wanted to fly again. After four months of grieving the loss of my helicopter, compounded by overwhelming anxiety, I overpowered my fears, and I've been back in the air for many months now. The first time I went up, I was terrified, but stepped into my fear. I went with an instructor, but I did all the work. At times, it felt like I was simply going through the motions, but I knew this would bring me to the other side of my fear.

Once I was flying, the fear began to subside, and I got my confidence back. It didn't take long. Most importantly, it made me get out of my head and back into my body. Action can cure debilitating fear.

It's too easy to forget about the power of our dreams when we are being driven by our fears. So here is the simple formula for overcoming your fears and stepping into your empowered life:

1. **Refocus on your dream.**
2. **Release the past.**
3. **Take action.**

You must make your dreams more important than your fears. When you feel yourself slipping away from the reason that started you pursuing your dream, you must re-engage that original FEELING that you had. This will help you get motivated and inspired again. It's easy to be excited until you are up against the big challenges that stand between you and your dream life. Your challenges are the tests you must pass to deserve your wishes. You really don't deserve the reward until you've passed the tests. You earn your dreams by solving the problems you are faced with on your journey to acquire them.

My favorite quote includes everything you need to achieve a wildly successful life: "Have a big dream. Work hard. See the job through." –Kenny Troutt, billionaire

I'm grateful every day for the days I didn't quit. I'm an experienced (but always learning) and humble licensed helicopter pilot and I get to give others the experience of first-time flight.

No matter how challenging the road ahead may seem, always stay focused on your goals and celebrate the progress you have already made. Take action on your dreams and always remember, you have the strength and ability to overcome any challenge that comes your way.

ABOUT JORDAN ADLER

Jordan Adler believes a big dream and a will to work hard and never quit is the secret to success. Jordan is one of the most highly paid network marketers in the world. Jordan lives his dreams on a big scale and inspires others to do the same. His best-selling book, *Beach Money*, has sold more than 1 million copies, and 100% of the profits of his book are donated to an organization that helps entrepreneurs in developing countries start small businesses through micro loans. He has been featured in over 100 books and has been a guest on more than 150 podcasts. He has spoken on stages with Richard Branson, Tony Robbins, Sean Whalen, Ed Mylet, Pitbull, and Eric Worre.

Watch this short video to hear Jordan's business building tip to success!

REFLECTIONS ON RESILIENCE

Have you ever felt held back by fear? I know I have. Sometimes, it can feel like our dreams are out of reach because we're too scared to take action. But the truth is, fear is a normal part of the journey toward achieving our goals.

From the moment I decided to write this book, I have had moments of fear and nervous thoughts. It can be really tough to push through that fear and take action. But let me remind you that you have pushed through fear before to get to where you are now, so it's totally possible to overcome new fears and achieve your goals.

Just look at Jordan's story: He wanted to fly helicopters, but he was faced with plenty of obstacles along the way. Despite all the challenges of learning a new skill, he pushed through the fear and worked hard to get his helicopter license. Even after he pushed through this fear to get his license and he started to fly, he faced another major setback—a terrible crash.

His story is a reminder that our challenges are just tests we need to pass to deserve our dreams. So, take a moment to think about your own goals and dreams. What are some things you've always wanted to do? Maybe it's starting your own business, reaching the next promotion or rank in your business, traveling to a new place, or learning a new skill.

Think about your goals and dreams and write them down below. It's amazing how much power there is in putting your thoughts on paper.

_____

_____

_____

_____

_____

_____

_____

Next, what's one small action you can take **right now, today,** to move toward one of your goals? It doesn't have to be a big leap—just a small step forward.

_____

_____

_____

_____

Always remember that fear is a natural part of the journey toward achieving your goals, and it's okay to feel scared. The important thing is to acknowledge your fears and take small steps **every day** toward your dreams. So, believe in yourself, take action, and make your dreams a reality.

Action breeds confidence and courage.
If you want to conquer fear, do not sit
home and think about it. Go out and
get busy.

–Dale Carnegie

CHAPTER 2

THE SEEDS OF BELIEF

Jimmy Dick

THE SEEDS OF BELIEF
Jimmy Dick

My early childhood was quite a contradiction. I'm dyslexic, and back in the early 50s when I started school, nobody really knew what dyslexia was, and they sure didn't understand it. For the most part, I was seen as a child who was borderline mentally challenged, not very smart. Thankfully, I had a few amazing folks around me, giving me all sorts of positive encouragement. But, on the flip side, there were a good number of people who weren't so kind, and they were also not shy about telling me they doubted my worth and ability.

36

Now, there are many forms of dyslexia, but the most common type means you struggle with reading and transposing numbers. And boy, did I struggle. It was only quite a bit later in life that I realized it was actually a gift. Dyslexics see the world differently, and if you're dyslexic, you know exactly what I mean.

When I was young, I was an absolute ball of energy, always getting into something. In those days, we didn't have kindergarten—one day you're killing bears and running with imaginary dinosaurs through the woods, and the next, bam! You're in first grade.

My first day of school was quite the experience. The teacher seemed sweet as pie, but as soon as the parents left, she turned into a dragon! I was in shock watching her write on the wall—I had never seen a blackboard before, and I never got to write on the walls at home. So, of course, I went up to try it myself, and what did I get?

Slapped on the head and dragged back to my seat. The teacher told me not to move, so as soon as she turned her back, I broke out of that jail and walked the two or three miles home. I told my parents I'd had enough of this.

And that, my friends, was the start of my educational journey. I fought the system for twelve years, never doing homework, but in the process also discovering my talent for math. I couldn't show the step-by-step process, but I could give them the correct answer, which got me accused of cheating until my dad stepped in. He explained that I couldn't show my work because I did it in my head. They insisted I needed to show the work. It was their way or no way.

I remember my fifth grade teacher telling the class, "Jimmy Dick, if you put your brains in a hummingbird, he'd fly backwards." And I remember saying, "They do fly backwards." I got grabbed by the ear again and off I went to the principal's office. Yeah, I hated school.

One thing that got me through my frustrating school experience as a very young child was a neighbor, a sweet little old lady who lived across the field from my grand-mother. Bedridden for years, she loved when I came over and told her my tall tales, about how I caught an eagle and rode on it, and how my dog Fido and I killed a bear.

She believed in me, encouraging my imagination and telling me to never let anyone crush my dreams. Many times I got punished for telling "lies," but she would stand up for me. She told my dad, "Don't you ever punish that child. He's not telling lies. He has a vivid imagination, and he'll amount to more than all the rest of them. One day, he's going to do something special."

She also told me, all the time, "Listen, baby, don't let them steal your dreams. You keep dreaming big. You keep telling your stories." She was a very powerful influence in my early life and I've carried her positive influence for decades.

But then there were the folks who just didn't get it that I still had to contend with. After high school, I joined the military to get away from all that. It was there that they discovered my true potential, and I was sent to radio tech school. I learned to read in my own unique way, realizing I had amazing retention skills.

When I got out of the military, I went to college and then university, got my master's in psychiatric social work, and even became a college professor. I became a director of a mental health center and taught in the graduate school of social work at the University of South Carolina. Being a college professor was a big move for a child who grew up with people telling him he was dumb!

Eventually, I left the mental health profession and went into marketing, and then into insurance and securities, and worked as a principal in a broker-dealer firm. I didn't really like the responsibility of the market shifting and moving. It meant when you made your clients money, you were a genius. And when the market went bad, you were to blame. So I sold out to my partners and went full-time into network marketing. And I'd finally found my passion.

I had dabbled in the profession as far back as 1958, but went full time into my first company in the late 80s. I've only been involved in five companies as a distributor or affiliate, or whatever the position was called. But I've been at the top of every company, from number one earner to number ten. I've made tons of money, but what I really loved was meeting people.

My entire working life, it's about sitting down, talking to people, connecting with them, helping them to identify their problem, whether that's in therapy or car sales or finding the right insurance or financial solution. I found it all tied together when I could offer someone an opportunity to create an extra stream of income through an MLM company on the side.

I've been invited to join a lot of opportunities, but for me to be involved in a business, they had to have three things. Number one is the people. Who are the people behind this company? What are their principles? What is their history, and how many companies have they started? Number two is the product. It has to be a product that brings value to the people I sell it to, and it has to be competitive in the marketplace. And number three is the opportunity, the compensation plan. But I never got to number three if the other two things weren't in place. Most people look at the compensation plan first, but I think that's backwards. It doesn't matter what the compensation plan is if the first two things aren't right. After many years, I've also come to learn that these three things, while very important, take a back seat to one other thing—and that's belief.

I love the quote from Henry Ford because it is all about belief. "If you think you can do a thing or think you can't do a thing, you're right." It's the most profound statement I've ever heard. Belief is the engine that drives a successful life. And when I say successful life, I'm not talking about accumulating a lot of wealth and material items. It's about celebrating life with people and making a difference while you're on that journey. So when you get to the end of your life, you can look back and say, "The world is a better place because I came this way."

Belief has been a strong guiding principle for me all of my life. I don't really recall having a bad day in my adult life when I wanted to quit on one of my goals, and I believe it's due to what that elderly neighbor kept telling me. I really believed her when she said I was special, even though I was getting a lot of negative input during school. You have to be careful what you tell a child, because they will believe what you say to them. If you tell them they are bad, they will act bad, and you'll have a problem. If you tell that child they're special and have a beautiful spirit, they're going to be somebody special and they will have a beautiful spirit. Her voice was the strongest for me.

When I look back at that, I really am puzzled by how her one voice of encouragement was able to overpower all the other voices of criticism. But she ingrained in me deeply by saying not to listen to people who said I can't do things, that told me I was dumb. She'd say, "Always believe you are special." And she'd grab my little cheek and kiss me on the head and say, "You are smarter than all the rest of them. You've got a brilliant mind."

I had so much exposure to her from age three to about six that she gave me very powerful and positive messages about myself. I think they were just strong enough to kind of override being told I was dumb.

So when I decided to go to college and learn, I did it. When I decided to get into a business, I did that. When I started a large financial services firm, I went to the top. Once I decide what I'm going to do, I go do it. When I decided I was going to work in network marketing, I didn't say I would "try" it. I made a decision to just do it.

One thing I encourage people to do is to stop using the word "try." I hear a lot of people say they're going to "try" to do something. That's a weak phrase. Use power words like do and know. **If you believe you can, you can. If you believe you can't, you can't. There's so much power in believing. It's everything. It's life.**

I do remember quitting something and that was smoking. Years and years ago, when I quit smoking cigarettes, I didn't "try" to quit. I quit. I took my cigarettes out of my pocket, laid them on the mantle, put the lighter there, and said, "I quit."

Jokingly, I told my wife not to move them, because if I ever wanted one, I'd know where they were. Five years later, when we sold our house, she said, "Can I throw these cigarettes away?" Making a commitment and taking action is not reserved just for business, it's life in general. If you're not going to commit to "do it," then don't do it.

There's a famous quote by Maya Angelou that has great significance for me: "People will forget what you said, people will forget what you did, but people will never forget how you make them feel." That's powerful.

You are in control. You are the master of what happens to you. You are 100% solely responsible for your failure and success. It's not fair to blame someone else. If you make a commitment and failure isn't an option, don't stop short of doing whatever you've decided you're going to do.

My story is proof that you are in control of your own life. So believe in yourself and always remember that you are special and have a beautiful spirit. Don't let anyone steal your dreams!

ABOUT JIMMY DICK

With over 50 years of experience in network marketing, Jimmy Dick is a highly accomplished professional in his field. He has consistently ranked at the top throughout his career, from being the number one earner to the tenth.

One of the things that Jimmy loves most about network marketing is the opportunity it provides for meeting and helping people. He believes in the transformative power of this profession and has made it his mission to help others achieve their goals. His impactful presentations and trainings have helped tens of thousands of people to achieve breakthroughs in both their personal and professional lives.

Belief has always been a guiding principle for Jimmy, and he has built his success on it. His unshakable faith has been the driving force behind his remarkable accomplishments.

Jimmy and his wife Kathy currently reside in North Carolina.

Check out Jimmy's video message for a powerful story on belief!

SCAN THE QR CODE

REFLECTIONS ON RESILIENCE

The words we use, both in our thoughts and spoken out loud, have tremendous power over our lives. Every day, we are constantly bombarded with messages from ourselves and others. These messages can be positive and encouraging, or they can be negative and defeating. Growing up, we may have received a mix of both kinds of messages, which can create a confusing and limiting internal dialogue. As Jimmy's story shows, it is possible to focus on the positive messages to create a foundation of belief in ourselves that can carry us through life.

To do this, we need to be intentional about the language we use when speaking to ourselves and others. We can start by asking ourselves whether the messages we tell ourselves on a daily basis are using language of success or language of defeat. Are we using power words as Jimmy calls them or success language, as I call it, to inspire ourselves to go after our goals? Are we asking ourselves empowering questions that can help us find solutions to challenges we face?

One powerful example of language we can change is the word "try." When we say we will "try" to do something, we are already giving ourselves an out, a way to not fully commit to our goal. The word "try" is a word of uncertainty. As Yoda famously said, "Do or do not. There is no try." Replacing "try" with "am" or "will" or "do" will make all the difference in how we approach our goals. As Jimmy shares, this small shift in language shows we are committing to our goals and taking ownership of our actions.

Another common phrase that holds us back is "I can't." This is a limiting belief phrase that takes away our control. By replacing it with "I choose not to," we acknowledge that we are making a choice and staying in our power. This can open up new possibilities and help us find innovative solutions to challenges we face.

By using success-oriented language and asking ourselves empowering questions, we can start to transform our internal dialogue and become more resourceful in achieving our goals. For example, instead of lamenting, "I can't take a trip this year," ask yourself, "How can I take a trip to (fill in the blank) this year?" This simple rephrasing can open up a whole world of possibilities and can help you find creative solutions.

This is not a one-time fix; it's a lifelong practice of self-reflection and intentional language use. Here are some other examples.

LIMITING LANGUAGE	SUCCESS LANGUAGE
Try	I will, I am, Do
If	When
Probably	I will, I am
I can't	I can, I choose to (focus on what you can do)
Impossible	Possible, How can I?
I'm not good enough	I am enough or I am good enough, and I can always improve
It's too hard	I can do hard things or I embrace challenges and find ways to succeed
Problem	Challenge, situation, opportunity
I don't have enough time	I have the time to get things done or I prioritize what is important to me
I'm not lucky	I create my own luck through hard work and persistence or I always win

Starting today, what's one limiting word or phrase you will eliminate? Write it in the space below and put a strike through it as you make this commitment to yourself. For example: ~~Try~~

_____

_____

What's the power word or success language you will use starting today to describe yourself and your goals? How can you use success language and empowering questions to overcome challenges you are facing? Write it in the space below.

_____

_____

_____

_____

By being mindful of the messages we tell ourselves and intentionally choosing language that empowers us, we can create a more positive and fulfilling life.

When we use language that limits us, we unknowingly give away our power and control. So, when we intentionally choose power words and success language, we take ownership of our lives and our success. By consistently using language that uplifts us, we can transform our thoughts, our words and our actions, and ultimately create a life that is not only fulfilling but also aligned with our true potential.

Your beliefs become your thoughts,
Your thoughts become your words,
Your words become your actions,
Your actions become your habits,
Your habits become your values,
Your values become your destiny.

—Mahatma Gandhi

CHAPTER 3

RISING ABOVE THE NOISE

Mike Dreher and Darren Ewert

RISING ABOVE THE NOISE

Mike Dreher and Darren Ewert

We both grew up in a time when kids could just vanish into the countryside for the day and play in nature. Boy, those were the days! Darren later became a trained nutritionist, and Mike worked in corporate sales and marketing. Both careers shifted after a while, and Darren moved into online marketing while Mike got into business coaching.

We were together for a couple of years before we decided to combine our talents. We wanted to create something epic. We started our business from the ground up, which allowed us to define the fundamentals that are most important to us—respect, integrity, and honesty.

Our company offers all the tools, training, and systems digital business owners need to run a successful online business. We focus on helping people who have always wanted to work for themselves, and crack into the online world by specifically offering them systems, training, support, and even curated products. They don't need to have any prior business experience, they don't have to be a technological guru—everything is broken down into easy steps they can do at their own pace. We have a community of online business owners that spans the entire globe and we have tens of thousands of members.

Being an entrepreneur can be daunting and personally exhausting, because you constantly find yourself dealing with new challenges and trying to overcome new hurdles. You'll find yourself not only second guessing yourself at times, but you'll probably also find yourself surrounded by loved ones who may doubt you as well! On the days you don't believe in yourself, or nobody around you does, our community will. We get it, because we're all in the same boat together. We love the saying, "if you want to go fast, go alone. But if you want to go far, let's go together!"

It's a little synchronicity that both of us also happen to have the type of personality that if someone tells us something is "impossible" or "can't be done," we'll go to the ends of the earth to prove them wrong. We're also resilient, which comes into play way more often than you might guess.

We've found the only difference between a successful business owner and an unsuccessful business owner is getting up when you're knocked down! It's dangerous to look at someone who you see as wildly successful and assume that they were unique or special. This achieves nothing except convincing yourself that you'll never be able to do the same!

Being a successful, married, gay couple who works together online and makes no secret of it certainly does generate a lot of online feedback. Some of this is incredibly and unexpectedly supportive, but of course, much of it isn't. Sadly, we still don't live in a world where everyone agrees that all human beings are equal and entitled to the same rights. When you combine this reality with what we call "keyboard courage" (the tendency of someone to say something to you that they would never have the audacity to say to your face)—well, you get some terrible insults thrown at you sometimes online. It is hurtful and can cause a wave of negative emotions, even when you know it isn't true.

The hard part of working online is that you're putting yourself out there for all the world to see—and judge. And there will ALWAYS be hard moments and bad days when we and you have complete strangers making completely unfounded judgements about us and posting some pretty awful things. This is actually something that we coach our digital business owners through, because it really does require a person to develop stoicism and confidence. Haters will be haters, but you get to decide how it impacts you.

We learned a long time ago that the more successful you become, the more jealousy that can instill in others—and that is their journey, not yours. Remember, they're acting the way they are because of self-doubt and fear. We actually have discovered the best way to take away their power is to disregard their pettiness and to become the best and most successful version of yourself. It drives them crazy!

We are so lucky that we each get to work with our best friend and twin flame. When one of us is having a really hard time, the other one always has their back. We remind each other of who we are and what we're capable of. We do not take this for granted.

The best strategy we've found is really just to keep perspective. When something bad happens, spend some time with it. Ask yourself, "How bad is this, really?" What is the worst-case scenario? How would you deal with that worst-case scenario? How likely is it to even happen? It's so easy to automatically experience that fight-or-flight reaction to something instinctively, but when that happens, take a deep breath, and think it through.

**Your perspective in life is everything -
so pay attention to it.**

It's true that some people are so busy judging our personal lives (two gay men who are happily married in a monogamous relationship) that they overlook the fact that we've helped thousands of people all over the world with our support and coaching. But we choose not to let this take over our focus—to overwhelm us and cripple our potential. What we have learned is that others only have power over us if we allow it. So instead of accepting someone telling us that we are inferior members of society, we prove every single day just how valuable we really are, and we earn respect.

We're living what many would call the dream. We have beautiful homes, friends, and family that we get to visit all over the world, and a career that allows us to help others create real change in the world. The community and business we have built has brought families back together again. Immigrants have been able to bring their parents and children from overseas to live with them. Spouses have been able to quit their jobs and spend their days with their partners. Children have been able to travel home to spend days with their parents. This is what it is all about. Money isn't anything unless you use it for a heart-centered purpose.

We also like to stay focused on our "why" during bad days. This keeps us focused on what's really important.

Mike's why: To ensure that no matter what happens, I, and those that I love, have options in life, and that we will be okay. I'm a child of the 80s. I remember double digit mortgage rates, and people all around us losing their homes and their livelihoods. I remember how much my parents sacrificed to ensure we didn't lose ours. They fought with everything in them—and more. Now it's my turn.

Darren's why: I've always been a BIG dreamer and very ambitious. Our system works to help others achieve their dreams, and when they achieve their dreams, we also achieve ours.

Take the time to connect with your why. Why is it important to accomplish your goals and dreams? And when you think you've found your why, take it 10 levels deeper. You need clarity and focus to ensure your success. You need to be so connected to why success in your business is important that **nothing** can stop you.

For example, we asked someone recently why they wanted to start this business. They replied, "So I can spend more time with my kids." So we asked them why that was important to them, and they looked at us like we'd lost our minds. But we pushed them to think about it. They came back with, "Because I feel like I'm failing them by not being there." When pushed harder, they answered, "Because when I was young, my parents weren't there for me. And then I made some seriously bad decisions that took me years to deal with—and I don't want my kids to ever have to go through what I did."

Without going into the details further, by the end of that discussion, the person is much clearer on why it is so important to have their business succeed. They will fight that much harder to make it happen. Now it's not just about dollars and cents. It's not just business. It is a crusade for the good of their children!

Darren: One of my favorite quotes is, "The best way to get what you want is to help others get what they want." I love this quote because it's a simple explanation of the fact that you can take care of yourself while also helping others. The two don't have to be mutually exclusive, as so many people think. Servant leadership doesn't mean giving up everything—it doesn't mean that you have to sacrifice everything you have for others to win. Many people seem to think that to help others comes at a cost. But I actually think it's the opposite: Servant leadership helps you learn who you really are and what is truly important to you.

Mike: My favorite quote is, "Life is a journey, not a destination." I first heard this quote while I was back-packing all over the world in my early 20s. It was one of the most exciting times of my life, and also a time when I was really discovering who I was and who I wanted to be. It's such a simple quote, but when I heard these words, they really hit me in the heart. At the time, my life was all about the journey, experiencing new things and meeting new people. But it was also about my inward journey, as I built the person that I wanted to be. The world is always so caught up in what others want. And thanks to the internet, it's dangerously easy to look at others and judge ourselves as inferior. We forget that life is only about the journey. I truly believe that the whole point of our existence on this earth is to learn and evolve personally.

Our individual journeys and careers have led us to create something truly meaningful together. By combining our talents, we've built a community and a platform to support and empower aspiring digital business owners around the globe. Our resilience and determination to prove naysayers wrong has enabled us to help tens of thousands of people achieve their dreams while staying true to ourselves. By staying focused on our "why" and embracing a servant leadership mindset, we've found that success and fulfillment can coexist. We've learned that life is about the journey, and we are grateful to be on this journey together, supporting one another and helping others achieve their dreams. As we continue to grow our community and our business, we will always remember the importance of staying true to ourselves and using our success to make a positive impact on the world.

ABOUT MIKE DREHER AND DARREN EWERT

Mike Dreher and Darren Ewert are influencers, visionaries and successful entrepreneurs. Darren and Mike combined their backgrounds and experience and together have created an online, international, mentorship community for people who want to build their own successful online businesses. They provide all the systems, training, and guidance to help new entrepreneurs achieve incredible results—regardless of their experience, background, or education—and they now have tens of thousands of individuals who attribute their success to this system and community. They are very proud that they have helped thousands to not only wake up to their potential, but also to create their own success stories.

Watch this video to hear Mike and Darren's helpful tip on how to stay focused and energized while working towards achieving your goals!

SCAN THE QR CODE

REFLECTIONS ON RESILIENCE

When you value the attributes of respect and kindness, it's difficult to deal with negative comments and judgment from others. It is important to remember that our worth is not determined by others' opinions of us.

After reading Mike and Darren's story, take some time to reflect on how you deal with judgment from others and how you can protect your sense of self-worth.

Consider a quality or trait you possess that makes you unique. How can you use this quality to build your sense of self-worth?

_____

_____

_____

_____

Think of a time when you received positive feedback or affirmation from someone you respect. What did they say to you? How did this make you feel? How can you use this positive energy to help you navigate difficult situations?

_____

_____

_____

_____

Remember that you are a valuable and unique individual, with qualities and traits that make you special. Speak kindly to yourself, especially when facing criticism or negativity from others, and always remember that you are worthy and deserving of love and respect!

You have within you right now,
everything you need to deal with
whatever the world can throw at you.

–Brian Tracy

CHAPTER 4

NAVIGATING ROUGH TERRAIN

Phebe Trotman

NAVIGATING ROUGH TERRAIN
Phebe Trotman

One of my favorite memories from my childhood was an ordinary day when I was about five years old, and I was home alone with my dad. He was telling me he wanted to move a bookshelf, but said he'd have to wait until one of his friends could come help him. I puffed up a little indignantly and told him I was sure I could help him move it!

"It's too heavy for us!" he said, but I reassured him we could do it together. Later, he told me I had this look in my eyes that told him I knew we could do it. And we did! After we moved it, I told him, "See, we did it now."

He wrote those words on an index card in our home office. Growing up, every time I was in our home office, I saw that constant reminder to believe in myself. I grew up believing I could accomplish whatever I put my mind to. It was also an early and important lesson and constant reminder to me that when we come together, we can accomplish big things.

Growing up in Coquitlam, British Columbia, with a brother four years my senior and cousins who are also older, I was very competitive. When we played board games, I didn't just want to keep up with them—I wanted to win! (I still do.) We used to play a lot of games and sports, and I also started to play community soccer at age 5. I started playing on an all-boys team and everyone else was Caucasian, so I really stood out. But I didn't want to just stand out because of the color of my skin or because I was a girl. I wanted to stand out because I worked hard and—you guessed it—I wanted to win! This early sports training has served me well over the years, as I have continued to play soccer through adulthood. I've also remained competitive with myself by wanting to do my very best in all aspects of my life, including pursuing excellence in building my business.

For the past 16 years, I've been an entrepreneur, so to say there have been "challenging days" is quite an understatement. But when you work as an entrepreneur, the good days are typically so incredible that you find it worthwhile to push through the bad ones.

It most often isn't just one thing on one day that makes it a tough day, it's usually a series of challenging moments and days, piling on all the associated emotions that are part of the challenges, that make a bad day even more difficult.

And there were so many compounding issues that made my bad day so much more challenging. It was September 2017. I was at a leadership retreat when my network marketing company announced a special "fast track to promotion" incentive for the month of October.

If you are new to network marketing, here's a quick overview. Often, networking marketing companies will have different promotion levels. You can compare promotion levels or ranks to the sport of martial arts and earning different color belts. So as an affiliate or distributor grows their business through purchases made by people they have referred to the company, a distributor can promote through the different ranks. Some companies offer an increase in earning potential or prizes when you hit new ranks. Network marketing companies also have their own compensation plan, which can have a variety of requirements to ensure a company is legal. To hit different ranks, companies may require you to create a certain amount of volume or sales in a given period. Companies may also only allow a certain amount of volume to count to make sure someone isn't promoting through multiple ranks by helping one person get started (a leg) and that's it.

Everyone at the retreat was so excited, as this incentive meant many people at the retreat would rank-advance. And we all knew it would also create excitement for our team members to rank-advance as well. When I first heard this announcement, I was two promotions away from the top level in the company, and I made the decision that I would promote those two ranks by the end of the next month. I was already almost at the next promotion level and figured out I only needed to do a couple of things to hit the first part of my goal, which I could do in a few days. I knew that October was going to be a "pray like it depends on God, work like it depends on you" kind of month. But I was excited! This would be a huge milestone month for my business and for many of my team members.

I went to work to complete the few things I needed to do to promote to the next rank, and I emailed our company's corporate team to confirm I had hit the second rank from the top, which they confirmed. Sweet! Knowing that was done, I focused on my next goal to hit the top rank, which meant I would promote twice in October. The president of our company at the time had always taught distributors to "know your numbers," so I was confident I had hit the second rank from the top.

The first Monday evening in October, the company corporate team was scheduled to hold its leadership call where they would announce the rank advancements and company updates. I was full of excitement, texting team members during the day to make sure they got on the call as the company was going to be announcing the "fast track to promotion" incentive. When the call was finished, I texted the company president to let him know how excited everyone on the team was about this incentive. I went to sleep thrilled, knowing I'd accomplished my rank advancement. The next morning, my phone was blowing up from team members and cross-line friends who were excited about the company incentive.

I was driving home from an early morning networking meeting when my phone rang, showing our company president's name on my screen. I answered excitedly, thinking he was calling to congratulate me on my promotion. But he told me instead that he had some bad news, and I didn't qualify for the promotion because of a 50% maximum leg split volume require-ment. I remember precisely where I was driving on Broadway Street when I pulled over in shock, disap-pointment, and frustration.

Even though I was deeply disappointed, we had a good pep talk and because it was early in the month, I knew I could still hit my double promotion goal. But the way the company's compensation plan worked back then, I had to hit this next promotion in the next few days, or I wouldn't be able to make my goal of double promoting. It was a Tuesday, and I was leaving for a conference, so I set my goal to hit it before I got on that plane on Thursday afternoon.

A few close team members were also working toward their own promotion, so I shared with them my new goal, and we all went to work. They knew if they hit their goals, it would help me with the first part of my promotion goal as well. We all worked hard over the next couple of days - early mornings and late nights following up with people we had previously shown our product and business opportunity to. I tracked every-thing, including numbers.

Boarding the plane, I was a little apprehensive, as I was still short of the volume needed to promote. Keep in mind, I'm usually the person who sleeps from takeoff to landing, but for the first time ever, I purchased Wi-Fi on a plane. One of my close friends and team mem-bers continued to send me messages of encouragement throughout the flight to keep going, so that's what I did.

I remember experiencing the worst turbulence ever and still helping people get started through iMessage. I landed for a short layover, and I prayed the work I did on the plane, along with my team's work, would create enough volume to hit my next rank. I called in to our corporate office and sure enough, they confirmed I'd done it—I'd hit the second rank from the top!

We had two big events coming up, so the local team was working hard to leverage these events and the excitement to help with promoting. We were all working non-stop to invite guests to the events while helping others get started with their accounts.

A nearby distributor and I joined forces to hold a contest for the first event, intending to invite the winners on a special call with our company's top income earner, along with our president of field operations. A few days before the winners' call, I asked the company for a breakdown of my current volume, since I couldn't see the leg split details in my business office online. When I got the numbers, I knew something was off. I realized an entire leg of volume wasn't included on its own and was incorrectly included in another leg.

What this error also meant was at the beginning of the month when I was told I didn't rank-advance with the promotion, I actually did, that day. So when I joined the winners' call, I felt disheartened. We were on the winners' call and the top income earner in my company shared a story in the last few minutes of the call that came at the time I needed it the most. His story reminded me there was still a chance, and it also reminded me of my dad always cheering me on and encouraging me to keep going. So I went back to work.

I shared the short audio clip with the story with my team leaders, as they were also frustrated at some hurdles we'd faced together during this month. The second event was days away, though, so we recommitted. We knew this was a chance to do something big for our businesses, our futures, and our dreams. We created a wave of excitement that was contagious. We had a group chat with team members, and even close friends who were not on our team, to cheer and encourage each other in these last few days of the promotion.

We all were 100% invested in helping one another hit our goals and we cheered like crazy when one of us got promoted. We had many promotions, which we celebrated at the second event. I was so excited as it was the end of October and I hit my goal of promoting to the top rank in the company. I had volume in multiple legs, I had all the qualifications needed, I saw the volume in my business office and I had done it!

A few days later, I got a call from the founder of my company who congratulated me on hitting the top rank, but said, unfortunately, four months prior I had purchased a gift account for a friend and therefore I would have to qualify again. To be clear, I didn't earn any income from this new account and it didn't impact anything that was happening in this month.

When he said I would have to qualify again this month in order for my promotion to stand, I was crushed. I was hit with the roller coaster of emotions again and a tsunami of tears—of anger, frustration, disbelief, and shock. Later that day, one of my good friends called to congratulate me on hitting my goal of the top rank, as she knew I was focused on this goal, but I shared with her the news that I'd have to do it again. I told her what had happened. I was done, exhausted. I would regroup and go for the promotion another time. She was the friend, coach, and mentor I needed at that moment. She told me that I was absolutely going to do it and reminded me of my why and who I am.

The next day, my company owner and company president called again to check in on me and see how I was doing, given how upset I'd been the previous day when they delivered the news. I told them, yes, I'm still upset and frustrated but that I was going to hit it again. I'm going to do it. My company owner said he was proud of me for how I was handling the situation and that he could see me one day telling this story from stage (well here we are!). Only a handful of people knew what was happening, and that I had to qualify for the top rank again.

I shared with some close team members that November was going to be an action-packed month as I wanted to keep the momentum going—which was true, but it was also because I had to do it all over again. It was another busy month, but I did it. I was in Barbados when I got the call from my company founder. It was December 13, and he said he was pleased to congratulate me on hitting the top rank in the company. They would be making the official announcement in January, but on their end, it really was official. I got off the phone once again with a torrent of emotions, thinking of everything I went through and what my team went through to get to this moment. For me, being in Barbados, one of my favorite places, made it even better. And yes, even with the confusion and disappointment, it was worth it.

One of the best things you can do to help you through challenging times is to find a tribe of people who will remind you of who you really are. Surround yourself with people who know who you are at your core. Find people who will speak into your life and be there in your corner, no matter what. Pour into them with positive words and support as they pour into you.

We have heard it before, but do you really have those people in your life? Not just to pat your back when things are going hard, or cheer for you when things are going well. They're also the ones who will tell you the honest truth and lift you up when you may not feel strong enough to lift yourself up. I'm fortunate to have a lot of people in my corner and what I learned during this challenging period is that it isn't just about having great people in your life: It's also about having great people in your life who have been through challenging days themselves so they understand the journey. They are the ones who will say, "You're right, it isn't fair, and you are going to do it anyway, because that's who you are and that's the goal you set for yourself."

I'm grateful I didn't throw in the towel that second month and even grateful for the challenging days throughout those couple of months because it reminded me of that little girl who believed in herself and confidently told her dad she could help him. I had to dig deep many times throughout the month and give myself the encouraging talk that I often would give team members when they were struggling. The days throughout that push to double promote challenged me to grow. There were so many celebrations throughout those few months and being able to celebrate team members was incredible. I've always loved being a part of a team and working with others to accomplish goals and celebrate them when we hit them. **I've learned that regardless of the obstacles that present themselves, by focusing on your goal and surrounding yourself with people who have your back, you truly can accomplish great things.**

The following spring at our Company Convention, I was recognized for hitting the top rank in the company and I was also presented with the Global Referral Partner of the Year Award. It was a huge moment for me, as it was something that I had thought about and written down when I attended my very first convention. I wanted to hit the top rank, and I wanted to win the Referral Partner of the Year award one day, so to receive both at the same convention was so special. It was even more memorable as my mom was at the Convention to celebrate with me and I had a chance to see many of the team members who worked so hard to promote in October recognized on stage as well for promoting in their businesses.

Pushing through that challenging time and not quitting helped strengthen my belief in myself. Thinking back on that moment and everything I went through gives me the confidence when pursuing other opportunities like writing this book and creating this book series. It has been a huge stretch for me, but I continue to focus on the goal of helping others and I know by sharing these stories it will help inspire others. Knowing the positive impact this book will have on others is the fuel I needed to keep going when faced with challenging days in finishing this book.

I love the quote by Confucius, **"Our greatest glory is not in never falling, but in rising every time we fall."** It reminds us we all are going to fall in life—that is part of taking risks and living life to the fullest and that's OK. To do anything great in life, we must be prepared to fall, and we must be prepared to take action to get back up.

It is with the rise that some of our greatest lessons are learned and it helps us grow into the person we are meant to be. This quote has helped me through my journey because I have fallen a lot, there have been many bumps in the road and challenges in life, and I know there are going to be more. This quote helps me remember to embrace challenges and rise from every  obstacle stronger and wiser so I'm more equipped and ready to face whatever comes my way.

ABOUT PHEBE TROTMAN

Phebe Trotman is a Vancouver-based entrepreneur and accomplished soccer player. She has achieved many accolades as an athlete, including being inducted into several sports halls of fame, winning championship titles, and being recognized as an exceptional athlete. Phebe has also excelled in her career as a network marketer, earning top awards and recognition within her company. She is passionate about personal growth and empowering others to reach their full potential.

An extra special video message full of gratitude and encouragement for you, from me!

SCAN THE QR CODE

REFLECTIONS ON RESILIENCE

After reading my story, take a few moments to reflect on your own journey. Are there people in your life who have been there for you through thick and thin, both personally and professionally? Who are those individuals that have supported and encouraged you when you needed it the most? It's important to note that your go-to people professionally may differ from your go-to people personally, and that's okay. Think about those individuals who have been there for you through the good and the tough, and who always have your back. List their names below.

Personally: Professionally:

_____   _____

_____   _____

_____   _____

_____   _____

_____   _____

It's important to not only recognize the value of these relationships, but to also show your appreciation for them. Take a moment now to express your gratitude to these individuals who you can rely on when you're having a tough time, whether it's through a text, voice or video message, a phone call, or a heartfelt card or letter.

Remember, relationships are a two-way street, and it's important to give as much (or more) as you receive. Think about ways you can support and encourage these individuals. Become their biggest cheerleader by celebrating their successes and be there to lend an ear when they need it.

But what if you don't currently have a strong tribe of people you can rely on? It's okay, and you're not alone. Building a supportive tribe takes time and effort, and it's worth it. Start by seeking out individuals who share similar interests or values as you. Join a church, find a club or organization, attend networking events, or volunteer in your community. Engage with others and be intentional about cultivating new positive relationships. Remember, look to give and positively pour into others first and in time, it will be reciprocated.

Building a strong community isn't just about having people who are there for you during the tough times. It's also about having a group of individuals who celebrate your successes and inspire you to be the best version of yourself!

We need to surround ourselves with
people who are going to lift us higher.

–Oprah Winfrey

CHAPTER 5

FROM HURT TO HEALING

Jen Furness and Jeanie Fountain

FROM HURT TO HEALING

Jen Furness and Jeanie Fountain

We are twins, born in South Korea but moved to the United States as toddlers with our 4'11" Korean mama in 1972. Our favorite childhood memories recall the simplicity of growing up in the 70s and 80s, when using your imagination and playing outside was natural and a part of our daily routine. We didn't have any technology or social media to crowd out our beautiful state of mind where we believed anything was possible.

Both of us were always athletes and competitiveness was second nature. We were the middle children, twins, with abounding ambition. Starting our grand adventure in network marketing was natural for us because TEAM was our whole life growing up playing basketball, volleyball, golf, and softball. Creating a collaborative, supportive community was already ingrained in us from the age of 10 (kids didn't start sports at age 5 back then!).

We both started our work lives as occupational therapists, which we did for more than 20 years. We dropped our kids off at daycare since they were six weeks old, worked 50+ hours per week and were always tired. We were always entrepreneurial and looking for ways to be our own "bosses," but always landed in the brick and mortar traditional business. We were never taught anything but employee and business owner mindsets. We really didn't see network marketing as a true "profession" and never imagined it would be the answer to our prayers!

Jen: I was introduced to network marketing via a random Facebook post, and after a few months of seeing compelling results, I demanded my twin sister's credit card, because who wants to do anything new and exciting without her best friend?

Our first year, I sponsored 10 people, and Jeanie sponsored five people into our businesses. We were so excited as we both became car bonus qualified and, seeing the success we had created, we were determined to help our teams do the same. Our occupational therapy company closed that year and I decided to focus on my business while Jeanie decided to get a job. My husband gave me an ultimatum of two months to make this successful, "or you're getting a real job." I won!

The next year, we continued to build our business and Jeanie cut back her hours to part time while I was all in. I even gave up my license to practice occupational therapy.

Jeanie: It was in our third year in our business when I joined Jen in "retirement" and left my job. We were sprinting together, focused on building our business and helping our teams grow. We experienced a lot of growth and made it to the top of our company.

We both continued to sponsor customers and people in our business and help our teams do the same. Just like all businesses, network marketing has its fair share of ups and downs.

Our worst day came about six years into building our business. It was the day we discovered the reality behind the saying, "Drama kills checks." Our teams were rapidly growing, and our systems were working. And then, gossip and de-edification amongst leadership seeped into conversations. That ONE conversation led to a virus that poisoned hundreds, maybe even thousands, of people on our team.

We had a team of about 7,500 when the ripple effect of the negativity and drama capsized our organization. Unfortunately, once the gossip was said, there wasn't anything we could do to undo the impact. People became discouraged and frustrated and many of our team who were building their businesses ended up being so negative that they quit the business. Most just became glorified customers because they still loved the products. However, they lost trust in the business model and no longer were building!

We lost faith in our trusted leaders and in the industry a little, too. Within network marketing, there is an unspoken standard to edify your team members. It is important to build with integrity and to build each other up. We lost that for sure, because of one conversation that led to many conversations. We felt betrayed, angry, frustrated and bitter for a while, while also just in disbelief at what was happening. We were shocked that our upline leaders would have acted this way, in a way that destroyed so much of the work we had done and they lost their businesses, too.

At the time, though, we couldn't imagine the pot could be poisoned like that. But network marketing is a people business. In transparency, the hurt caused some "woe is me" feelings for a few days (or months or years). But we prayed and asked God to make a way and to stay the course.

It did take some time to move forward, but thankfully the feelings of disappointment have cleared. We refused to allow the enemy to get a foothold and steal our joy. We believe and know we serve a big God who is our front guard and rear guard and that's why we didn't quit on a bad day, weeks, or years. His faithfulness fortified our grit on that bad day. We know we can use our gifts and talents to continue to serve others and to move forward in spite of outside circumstances and people.

We are now actually grateful for that day because it taught us that when we humble ourselves, regardless of the intentions of others, we are still blessed. We can still make our way forward. We feel blessed beyond reason—

stronger and wiser. We're not where we want to be, but we are thankful we are not where we used to be!

We have grown so much. Our transformations, emotionally and spiritually, have been staggering. We spent nearly two decades believing our careers were the only way to provide. Now, we realize more than ever, true success and fulfillment are discovered in service to others.

Our ability to impact the world has grown exponentially. Because we didn't quit on that bad day, we have been able to retire our husbands. We have set an example for our kids and grandkids that our envisioned lives drive our real lives.

We built our network marketing business for 11 years. Now, we own a holistic mind body wellness facility, and we're on a mission to bring healing to a nation in desperate need. As Earl Nightingale said, "We become what we think about." This is powerful and something to ask yourself on a daily basis. What are you thinking about? Is it serving you? If not, are you willing to let it go?

- What we think about we will find.
- What we think about grows.
- What we think about seems real.
- What we think about, we become.

Because we didn't quit on that day, we have true freedom and flexible lifestyles to spend time with our kids and family traveling the world. Heck, we never even had passports until we became entrepreneurs.

If your current life is not taking you to your dream life, MOVE! As Jim Rohn always said, "You're NOT a tree!" Life is too short to live in black and white: True purpose and fulfillment are only found in FULL COLOR! Other people's blessings are tied to our obedience! What are you waiting for? There are people out there waiting for you and the positive impact and blessing you can be in their life. When you shine, you give others permission to shine as well!

ABOUT JEN FURNESS AND JEANIE FOUNTAIN

Jen & Jeanie are twins, Jesus-loving, Light-shining, entrepreneurs. They were occupational therapists for more than 20 years, network marketers for 11 years, and now owners of Boundaries Mind Body Wellness, a wholistic mind body wellness facility on a mission to bring healing to a nation in desperate need.

Take a look at Jen's empowering video message on navigating life's struggles!

REFLECTIONS ON RESILIENCE

Jen and Jeanie's journey teaches us about the power of faith and forgiveness. It's common to feel disappointed and frustrated when someone we trusted lets us down or when someone else's drama causes us pain.

Despite the hurt they experienced, Jen and Jeanie were able to trust in God to help them forgive those who hurt them and continue using their talents to help others. Have you ever experienced the healing power of forgiveness in your own life? What positive outcomes did it bring?

_____

_____

_____

_____

Let's also take a moment to reflect more about our own gifts, and how we can use them to make a positive impact on the community around us. Even in difficult circumstances. What are some of your talents and strengths? List them below.

_____

_____

_____

_____

_____

Remember, we all face challenges and disappointments in life, but we have the power to choose how we respond to them. By practicing faith and forgiveness and using our gifts to serve others, we can find the strength to move forward and make a difference in the world.

Forgiveness is not an occasional act;
it is a constant attitude.

–Martin Luther King Jr.

CHAPTER 6

TURNING ADVERSITY INTO OPPORTUNITY

Steve Schulz

TURNING ADVERSITY INTO OPPORTUNITY

Steve Schulz

From a very young age, I understood the concept of entrepreneurship. The little town where I grew up, Wisconsin Dells, Wisconsin, had a population of about 2,500 people. But in the summer, it swells to as many as 100,000 people, all at once.

At 12 years old, I was already working 40 hours per week during the summer. I remember thinking, "What if all these people were coming to MY business?" Working for other business owners, even at that young age, made me realize I wanted to be the boss and call the shots. I knew that someday I would own my own business and create something many people would enjoy coming to. Spoiler alert, it happened!

Although I am ultra-competitive in sports, the only person I ever competed against in business was myself. To this day, I set goals and create strategies to achieve those goals, and I don't expect anyone to give me anything. It's my job to take care of my family and make sure that they have everything they need. My success in business is the determining factor in making that a reality. I am not in competition with anyone except my commitment to my family. Knowing I can always help my children with their college education or a down payment  on a house is a great feeling, but none of that happens if I'm not successful in business.

Despite my early thoughts of being my own boss, I didn't start my work life as a business owner. Most of us are taught at an early age to work hard in school, work hard in college, work hard at our 9 to 5 day job, and be grateful for two weeks of vacation per year. The idea is that if you work hard for many years, you can eventually retire and enjoy life.

Like many others, I set off on that path by working as a fifth-grade teacher. After spending a few days in the teacher's lounge, I figured out I'd been given a "bill of sale" on that "hard work equals a charmed life" thing! I saw teachers in the lounge who had taught for 30 years and all they did was complain. I knew I needed to look for something where I was the boss.

One Sunday night, a friend of mine introduced me to an opportunity that changed my life. For a $400 investment, I learned I could open my own home-based business and make money by asking people to switch their phone service. This was back in 1990, before the days of cell phones or the internet. I wavered back and forth on the business idea with my friend for two hours. There was a lot of doubt, many unknowns, and a lot of "what if's."

My wife Colleen grew tired of us talking. "For $400, what if it works?" she said.

That little spark of encouragement was all I needed, and it was a decision that would change our lives. I dove headfirst into the business. The journey was not an easy one in the beginning. My first check was less than a dollar, but I was ecstatic—not because of the amount, but because of what it represented. I knew the system was in place and what I was doing was working!

Ironically, despite Colleen's initial enthusiasm, she found it difficult to watch me work so hard for so little gain in the beginning. Despite the many ups and downs, I was looking ahead at the long-term benefits of my efforts. I believed that if I planted enough seeds for a few years, I would reap the harvest down the road.

The harvest turned out to be something we couldn't even fathom at the beginning. Not only did the harvest bring in multi-millions of dollars, but after three years working in my business, I was able to retire from my teaching position at age 29, which brought in the freedom to spend precious time with my young family.

I worked hard every day to get my business to a point that created a residual monthly income that was larger than most people made in a year. After a while, my business was on autopilot. I had hundreds of people joining my team monthly. These were people I didn't know, nor did I have to manage them. My life was incredible. I was my own boss. I called the shots. I set my own schedule. I never missed my children's games, concerts, or events. I was teaching thousands of other people how to do the same and speaking to groups of 10,000 people at a time.

Now, I don't want to say that everything was perfect, but it was darn close! I had challenges in building my business, but it was nothing I couldn't overcome. Or so I thought.

The most challenging day I ever faced was the day I learned the company I had been with for 14.5 years was closing its doors. I had put my heart and soul into building a company inside that company. I was an independent representative, and the company quit me. I didn't quit them.

We had just built our dream home—a 13,000-square-foot masterpiece that had EVERYTHING! The day we closed on that house was the day we were told our income from this company was ending.

Not good! I had a few choices. I could get mad at the company and blame them for everything, or I could look at the situation as a new door opening for me to create a new opportunity.

I loved the industry I was in. It wasn't the industry's fault that the company failed. Many others in the failed company blamed the industry and left it for good. I never understood that thinking. In business, companies fail all the time. It was no different in the network marketing industry. The difference was, the network marketing industry gave me the chance to hit home runs financially. Working for someone else in a "traditional" business gave me the opportunity to hit singles and build someone else's dream.

There was no decision to be made here. I was staying in the network marketing industry. I just needed to find a new vehicle. I did just that and continued to build my team. That was 18 years ago. I'm still swinging. I will decide when it's over.

I learned a very important lesson the day that company closed its doors. The lesson was simple. Even though the company I was building with was gone, I was still in business. How could that be? Because my team was intact. Life is nothing more than building relationships and sharing ideas. The relationships were still there. People will do business with people they know, like, and trust. **The more quality relationships you build, the richer you become. If you can surround yourself with people you like and trust, your earning potential becomes unlimited.** My success is not predicated on the product I promote. My success is measured by the company I keep!

People ask me all the time, if I could go back and change something, what would that be? My answer is always the same: I'd change absolutely nothing, because everything that has happened has gotten me to where I am today.

Trust me, I've wanted to quit a thousand times. I used to think, how many roadblocks can I possibly go through? What always got me through rough patches was me asking myself, what else are you going to do? Are you going to go back to teaching school? I knew that wasn't an option. The moment I found out my former company was closing, I thought the sky was falling. My income was immediately cut off, and I had just purchased a $3 million home. Looking back, it was necessary for that to happen so I could open other doors and become more successful than I was in my first 14.5 years in business.

Adversity is preparation for greatness. Your comfort zone is actually the most uncomfortable place to be. When you are comfortable and not stretching yourself, you can't grow. I know this sounds crazy but being uncomfortable is where I like to be. It challenges me to be better. It works for me 100% of the time!

Today, I am building a multi-million-dollar international company and I am making more money than at any time in my career. I am helping more people succeed than ever before. I'm traveling around the world meeting amazing people. None of that would have happened without adversity. That dark day turned out to be the best thing that ever happened to me in business. It allowed me to become much more open-minded and be aware of opportunities all around me.

I look for inspiration that I can share with my team every day. Inspiration is everywhere, you just need to know where to look. Many times, we are in the right place at the right time. As a matter of fact, you reading this right now means you are in the right place at the right time. There is an opportunity waiting for you. The problem is most people don't recognize it. Always be aware and open-minded to opportunities that come your way.

A quote I use as a learning tool for my team is one of my own, "If you can't keep up, take notes." I know that might sound harsh, but I became so tired of people in my organization complaining that "it's not working for me" that I decided to make a point and lead by example. I wasn't going to drag anyone across the finish line of success. I was going to show them the way. It was up to them to follow the path. It was also up to them to keep up and keep learning!

I have taken my own advice with that quote. I don't know everything, and each day is a new opportunity to learn and grow. I watch other successful people and mimic what they are doing. I sift through their techniques and apply them to my business and make them my own. You don't need to reinvent the wheel, but you can make it better!

I faced challenges and setbacks, but I persevered and built a successful multi-million-dollar international company. Through it all, I learned that adversity is preparation for greatness and that being uncomfortable challenges me to be better. My advice to others is to be aware and open-minded to opportunities, always be watching and learning, and never stop striving for success.

ABOUT STEVE SCHULZ

Steve Schulz has been working in the networking industry for 32+ years. When he was first introduced to the industry, he was a full-time school teacher, not making enough money to do the things he wanted to do financially. After working his business part-time {3-5 hours per week} for about a year, his wife Colleen left her teaching position and about a year and a half later, Steve left his. Over the past 32+ years, he built an organization of more than 200,000 Independent Representatives and has earned more than 20 million dollars. His mission is to mentor millionaires as he travels the world, training a simple system of success. He is also the author of the book, *Yes, Sometimes It Is About The Money.* Today he lives in Oconomowoc, Wisconsin.

Watch this video for a personal message from Steve that will lift you up!

REFLECTIONS ON RESILIENCE

Have you ever found yourself suddenly thrown off course, completely unprepared for what comes next? It can be a scary and overwhelming experience, but it's one we all inevitably face at some point in our lives.

Steve didn't let his company closing after 14.5 years stop him in creating a dream life for him and his family. Instead, he took control of the situation and made a conscious decision to move forward. By choosing to focus on the positive aspects of his previous experience, he was able to continue in network marketing with a new company where he created even more success.

I want to challenge you to reflect on your own experiences of unexpected pivots and adaptations. What's one time in your life when you had to make a quick change of direction? And more importantly, what did you learn about yourself during this experience? Take a moment to write it down below and see what insights you can uncover about yourself.

_____

_____

_____

_____

_____

_____

What positive outcomes came out of this unexpected pivot? Did you discover any new opportunities, strengths, or skills that you wouldn't have found otherwise?

_____

_____

_____

_____

_____

_____

Life is unpredictable, and unexpected changes are inevitable. It's how we respond to these changes that defines us. Embracing the unknown and being open to new opportunities can lead to amazing outcomes, personal growth, and transformation. By staying resilient and adaptable, we can turn even the most challenging situations into stepping stones toward a better tomorrow!

Pivoting is about being able to
recognize and seize new
opportunities, even if they don't
fit within your original plan.

–Reid Hoffman

CHAPTER 7

THANKFULNESS IN TOUGH TIMES

Dave and Roxanne Obiso

THANKFULNESS IN TOUGH TIMES
Dave and Roxanne Obiso

Both of us grew up in the Philippines and we migrated as teenagers to Canada, along with our families. We were both very close to our families and spent a lot of time playing and learning things with our siblings. We met in 2007.

Our inspiration behind pursuing success in business is to help retire Roxanne's parents (Dave's parents passed away at a young age). The dream of retiring Roxanne's parents was born when we saw a business opportunity showing we can earn more through business, not just through a corporate job. Roxanne's parents gave up their beautiful life in the Philippines—their home and careers—for their children to have a better life, because in the Philippines, it can be difficult to find a job even with a college degree.

We are a great match because we're both dreamers. We want to have a better life and we always knew there was something more for us, where we can help a lot of people. But we didn't know how.

If you're going through a rough patch yourself, you may be able to relate to our worst day. Having come out on the other side, we truly believe that challenges are a part of life, but they don't have to crush you. In fact, they can make you stronger.

The exact date of our worst day was February 1, 2018. It was the day we received 30 days' notice to vacate the apartment we had been living in rent-free as resident managers for nearly nine years. Needless to say, we were not at all prepared for this news! After we got over the shock, we tried to see the silver lining in the situation, to believe it was a blessing in disguise, that God was pushing us to move on to the next chapter in our lives.

During the time we were resident managers, we had been building businesses, one after the other. Some lasted three years before they failed, and others just a few months. When we counted, we realized we had failed in more than 24 businesses. We tried real estate investing, buying and selling cars, network marketing, high yield investment programs, cash gifting, affiliate marketing, a social media agency, insurance, and others. Not only did we fail in so many businesses, we accumulated over $86,000 in debt in the process. Given all of that, to also lose our home was devastating. We hadn't saved any money during those nine years, and we had quit our full-time jobs because we wanted to work full-time in our business.

We considered going back to live with Roxanne's parents or with Dave's brother to start over. We were so lost.

But we know that tough times can also be a catalyst for personal growth. We're grateful for our personal development journey because we were able to shift our mindset and emotions and practice gratitude and faith. We knew this was just temporary. We started to count our blessings and declare God's promises over our lives.

We also affirmed over and over what we wanted to happen in our life. We even made a video documenting our worst day and proclaimed our desire to earn over $500,000 in one year. In that same year, after many months, we found the online business we are working in right now.

We humbled ourselves and went back to work with full-time jobs. In addition to these jobs and the online business we were doing on the side, we also had a cleaning job and rented our second bedroom to pay off our debts and help us run our business. We were dedicated to journaling what we were grateful for, and wrote down the blessings we were receiving from the situation. And we also always thank God in advance for what we want to happen as if it has already happened.

We sacrificed a lot because we knew we were (and are!) building something for Roxanne's parents and our life and family. We knew our challenging circumstances would only be for a short time. We had our eyes on the long-term prize of time and money freedom. We didn't make the $500,000 after one year, but we did attain our goal in our third year in the business.

We're now very grateful for that day and those tough times because they pushed us to grow more and to expand more. We didn't know how small we were thinking at that time. We learned that we are more than capable of earning more and pursuing our dreams faster than we ever thought we could.

We also realized that if we had been blessed financially sooner, we would not have been ready. We didn't know how to manage our finances at that time. We learned that if you can't handle what you have, you won't be given more.

That day was our "never-again" moment. We don't ever again want to be in that same situation where we were not ready financially. We wasted nine years of not saving money and not taking good care of our finances. We learned that to become financially free includes managing your resources very well.

When we took full-time jobs again, we were on the verge of quitting our dreams of entrepreneurship and just settling for climbing the corporate ladder. But we continued to remind each other of our dream to retire Roxanne's parents and to have time and financial freedom. As a result of not quitting, we're completely debt-free.

After working in our online business, Dave was able to become boss free after 14 months and Roxanne after 29 months. We were able to buy our home, new furniture, fund our IVF treatment, give more to our church and ministries, treat Roxanne's parents and families to places and experiences, and travel—all without worrying about bills. We're now at a place of positive net worth and in a position to soon help Roxanne's parents in their retirement.

Having financial peace is a great feeling! We have two favorite quotes that we turned to often in our challenging times. One is, "If God is your partner, make your plans BIG!" by D.L. Moody. The other one that also really spoke to us is by Dave Ramsey: "If you will live like no one else now, later you can live and give like no one else!"

Hanging on to these quotes and beliefs helped us to stay focused, stay the course, remain committed, and never give up despite our trials.

Because we sacrificed for over 10 years building our dreams through businesses and not giving up, we are now experiencing this beautiful and blessed life and we give all the glory to God for all of it. We could not have done great things without Him—He directed us to people and resources that helped us get where we are.

If you're going through a tough time, we want you to know that better days are ahead. God has an amazing plan for you, and your current circumstances do not determine your future. So, believe in yourself and your abilities, and stay focused on your goals. Keep pushing forward toward your dreams, and with persistence and hard work, you'll accomplish incredible things!

ABOUT DAVE AND ROXANNE OBISO

Dave and Roxanne Obiso are online business coaches, mentors and trainers in the social media space, providing the tools, systems, training, and products to help people start an online business.

Dave and Roxanne's message is full of positivity and hope - watch and feel inspired!

REFLECTIONS ON RESILIENCE

Expressing gratitude, even during challenging times, is important because it helps to shift our focus away from the negative aspects of our situation and onto the positive aspects of our life. Positive emotions, such as gratitude, help you deal with stress better. It will also help to renew your creativity so you are better equipped to deal with challenging situations. Dave and Roxanne's story is a great example of this. Despite facing difficulties, they were able to find gratitude in their struggle, as they knew something better was on the other side of their challenging day. They knew they would come out stronger, they knew God had a bigger plan for them, and it inspired them to push through to create a better future.

Take a moment to think about your life. In the space below, write ten (or more) things, no matter how small they may be and people that you are grateful for. It could be anything from having a supportive friend to enjoying a cup of coffee in the morning.

_____   _____   _____

_____   _____   _____

_____   _____   _____

_____   _____   _____

_____   _____   _____

How do you feel now after thinking about and writing down things and names of people who you are grateful for?

_____

_____

_____

_____

_____

To make sure I'm intentional about expressing gratitude daily, I have a daily reminder on my calendar. Every day at 9:10 p.m., an event reminder pops up on my phone that says, "I am so happy and grateful that...". This helps me pause and take a moment to reflect on all that I'm grateful for that day and in that moment.

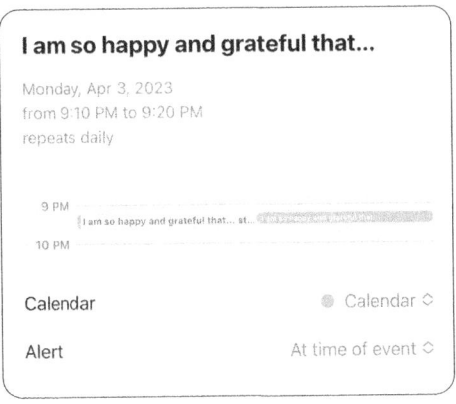

Remember, expressing gratitude not only makes us feel good, but it also helps us stay positive and focused on accomplishing our goals. By shifting our focus toward the positive, we attract more positivity into our lives.

As a bonus exercise, take a moment and record a short video to capture this moment. Perhaps you feel like you're not quite where you want to be yet and that's okay. We've all been there. Recording this moment for yourself now will allow you in the future to look back on where you started, see your progress and celebrate how far you have come. It's a powerful exercise that will remind you of the good things in your life and, just like Dave and Roxanne, it will help you stay positive and motivated.

Check out Dave and Roxanne's video from 2018 when they captured their tough day on video.

SCAN THE QR CODE

So, no matter what challenges you may be facing, remember that gratitude is a powerful tool that can help you shift your focus. Expressing gratitude and living a life of thankfulness is an essential component of building a strong foundation to persevere through life's challenges. By cultivating a grateful heart and focusing on the good in your life, you'll be amazed at what you can achieve.

Your current situation does not
determine your future. Your future
is determined by your decision
to succeed.

–Tony Robbins

CHAPTER 8

REFRAME YOUR DAYS

Scott Pospichal

REFRAME YOUR DAYS

Scott Pospichal

When I was about 11, my family moved from Wisconsin to Auburndale, a small town in Florida. Like a lot of 11-year-old boys, I loved football, and so I tried out for the little league football team. I was the last kid cut—I didn't make it. I was devastated. When my dad picked me up, he could see the devastation on my face. Not only had I just moved in, I felt like they didn't really give me a fair chance because they didn't know me.

Then the next week they called and said a kid had quit. Would I like to come back and try out for the team again? And I had to have a blocking competition against this other kid to see who made the team. I out blocked him, made the team, and ended the season as a cornerback and team captain. The next year I became a running back.

Getting cut was devastating, but also a great life lesson in humility and not giving up. When they offered me a chance to come back, I wasn't prideful and didn't keep my head down. I said, "Oh no, I want to come back! I want to be on the team." This helped me realize, even at a very young age, that something positive can come from tough stuff.

I played a lot of sports growing up and basketball was my favorite sport. Playing basketball in college was one of my goals. I walked on at Florida Southern my sophomore year. I was the twelfth man on the team, which meant I didn't get a lot of playing time. That year, we won the national championship.

When the season was over, I was working out in the gym when the coach came in and told me I should transfer. "I don't think you'll ever play here," he said. "You're a national champion. Why don't you go some-where you'll play?" And I told him no, I would stay and prove to him I could play. The next year I went from being the last guy to being a starter seven games into the season and went from being a walk-on to earning a scholarship.

So, I've never been much of a quitter. If I decide to do something, I find a way to do it, come hell or high water.

One challenge did almost get to me, though. In 1994, I was working as the basketball coach at Palm Beach Junior College in West Palm Beach, Florida, and building a network marketing business on the side. One of my prospects, a guy I thought could build a big busi-ness, asked me to come up to Orlando and he would fill up a room with prospects for me. Now, Orlando is almost three hours north of West Palm Beach. But my "I can do this!" nature agreed. Then he asked if I could pay for the meeting room. Well, sure, I agreed. I paid for the room in advance. And there's another guy who just joined my business, a very sharp guy. He said, "Coach, can I ride up with you?" I said, sure. So my wife (now my ex-wife) was giving me a really hard time. She said, "What are you going all the way up there for? You know no one is going to be there. And the weather is supposed to be horrible."

Well, the weather was horrible, but I drove almost three hours in a Florida downpour, pelted by wind and rain the entire drive. I got there early with my new buddy, the sharp guy who asked for a ride, and we got dinner at the hotel restaurant, which I also paid for. When it was closer to the meeting start time, my new team member, and I went up to the meeting room and not one person was there. Not one, including the guy who set up the meeting for me, who told me if I rented a room, he'd fill it for me. Nope. It was only the two of us.

I'm thinking, "There must be a reason this has happened." And then, I'm thinking sarcastically, "I can't wait to get home so my wife can say, I told you so." This was in my early phase of building my business, where you don't always see a lot of return. But this did seem over the top. Disappointed, we drove back home and just as I'm about to drop my new friend off at his car, he said, "Coach, listen. I'm in trouble. I need $400 to pay my child's support." I reached into my pocket and found $415. So I gave him $400.

Keep in mind, I wasn't doing well. I was in my third month of building my business. My first month I'd made $197 and the second month I made $837. But that can be inspirational to someone who doesn't have a lot of money. And so this was my third month. The hotel meeting room cost $175, but I chose to do it.

I got home a little after midnight and my wife was waiting for me. "How did the meeting go?" she asked.

"You wouldn't have believed it. It was packed. Amazing. I'm so excited about this guy. I'm so glad I went," I told her. I know that wasn't the truth, but sometimes it's important to look for the good, even though it's really hard to find sometimes. I wasn't going to let this guy's lack of keeping his word or my wife's negativity keep me from achieving my success. Even driving up from West Palm Beach to that ill-fated Orlando meeting, I told the man riding with me that it was cool to get to know each other, and we could schedule some meetings, and I would work with him and mentor him. But after I gave him the $400 (which, of course, I never got back), I never heard from him again. And I just said, "OK, next."

And I know that not every day is a good day. When people feel like there's a lot of stress around them, I say, "Hold it. Stop. Let me ask you a question. Are you healthy? Are your loved ones healthy?" I remind them to keep stress in check and stop worrying about the days that are less than great.

Even though I was extremely disappointed with that guy not showing up, I decided I was just going to keep working at it and continued to build my business. I had a full-time job, taking home $3,600 a month, and after a few months, I was making $1,500 in network marketing. I kept working my business and my checks continued to increase. The next month, I made $3,500 in my home business, and $9,200 the month after. When I got that check, my wife asked, "Do you think this company can afford to continue to send us all of this money?"

That check was the answer to every prayer on earth at the time. And I said, "I don't know but I can promise you one thing: I will work really, really hard as long as they can and until they stop." And during the time I was in that company, I made $4 million and changed the entire dynamic of how I've lived the next 30-plus years of my life.

Keep in mind, we weren't poor. I was making a good salary at the time. But when you see other families who have cool things and don't go to their mother-in-law's home for vacation every year, when you see people flying here and there for vacations while we drove everywhere, it can really motivate you to earn the things you want to do in life. We bought a second home on the ocean in New Smyrna Beach, Florida. And when we wanted to go on vacation, we'd drive the 170 miles from West Palm Beach to stay in our oceanfront, two-story, four-bedroom home. And if we wanted to go somewhere else, we could.

The owner of the network marketing company I was working in offered me a job to be a basketball coach for his youth basketball team; the Texas Titans. He moved my family to Dallas and paid me around $400,000 a year to coach youth basketball. We won eight national championships and put three first round draft picks in the NBA. This led to me meeting Avery Johnson, who offered me the chance to be his assistant coach at the University of Alabama.

Networking marketing is all about relationships, but one of the other mantras I hear a lot is about becoming like the people you spend time with. To paraphrase, show me your five best friends and I'll show you how much money you made. It just opens up a whole different lifestyle.

Network marketing is such an amazing industry. It's allowed me to follow a tradition my dad started when I was a child. He used to buy tennis shoes for the kids on our team who didn't have enough money to buy them. I didn't know about this when I was young, and only found out about it later in my life.

At a funeral one time a guy came up to me and told me, "Your dad's the one who always bought my shoes when I was in high school, when I couldn't afford them." I was blown away! I had no idea. Another one told me the same. Neither one knew who bought the shoes until one day the coach told one of them, "You know, Mr. Pospichal put shoes on your feet so you could play. Now play!"

Well, then it became my mission when I was speaking at meetings and if I'd see a young child there with their mom or dad, I'd say, "Do me a favor, let's get your mom (or dad's) phone and go to nike.com. I'm a shoe guy and I want you to find a pair of shoes you think are really cool. And after the meeting, I want you to come show them to me. But while we're in the meeting, you have to be quiet, OK?" And after the meeting, they'd bring me back the shoes they liked, and we ordered the shoes, and I paid for them. I've probably done this a hundred times. It made me feel good, and like I was continuing what my dad had started. It makes me happy and proud to continue this tradition.

In sports, as in business, you have to work hard. There is no other way. One of the quotes I used to put on the back of my youth basketball clinic t-shirts is, "The will to win is the will to work." Because you're not going to win if you don't work at anything. You have to make an effort. Especially in network marketing, you don't just find someone to be on your team who is a natural builder. You have to work at looking for that person, and then mentor them. But I promise you, **anything worth having in life is worth working for.**

One of my favorite quotes is, **"You think the price to pay is too high for success? Wait till you get the bill for regret."** This quote has always stuck with me as I remember in my early network marketing days, I was sitting on the floor at a Dallas Mavericks game with the owner of a former network marketing company, the one who hired me to coach his youth basketball team.

He has four floor seats, and he also has a suite. I asked, "Hey, how expensive are these seats?" He told me they were $1,500 each. And he has four, each game. I said, "Well, that's a heavy price!" And he pointed all the way to the top of the stadium and said, "Well, look up there. I believe they pay a  greater price to sit there because they're not willing to do what it takes to sit right here, close to the action." The point was, he was willing to do more to have more.

From being cut from a football team to building a successful network marketing business, I learned the value of not giving up and pushing through challenges. Success requires effort, and the price of regret is far greater than the price of hard work.

ABOUT SCOTT POSPICHAL

Scott Pospichal is an accomplished network marketing leader. After realizing he wanted more financial stability and personal freedom, he discovered the world of network marketing while working a full-time job and coaching basketball. He quickly made a name for himself in the industry and has since become a top leader, helping countless others build successful businesses.

One of Scott's greatest strengths is his ability to lead by example. He is known for his tireless work ethic and positive attitude, and is always willing to go above and beyond to support his team. He truly cares about the success of his fellow network marketers and is committed to helping them achieve their goals.

Scott's energy and enthusiasm are infectious, and he has a natural talent for motivating and inspiring others!

Tune in to Scott's video message and discover how a new perspective can change your life.

SCAN THE QR CODE

REFLECTIONS ON RESILIENCE

One thing that really stood out to me about Scott's story is that it took him some time to remember a day where he wanted to quit; he doesn't remember having many bad days because he always looks to find something good in his challenging days.

Think about a few of your own "bad days", even if you have to go back a long way like Scott did. What made those days tough? Was it something that happened at work, in your business, in your personal life, or something else?

Can you reframe those bad days by looking for the good in them? What did you learn from those tough times? Did they help you grow or become stronger in some way? Maybe you learned a new skill, made a new connection, or became more resourceful in some way.

This exercise might not be easy, but it's a great way to challenge yourself and see things from a different perspective. By finding the good in our bad days, we can learn to approach life with a more positive outlook.

So, take some time to reflect on one of your own bad days and see what you can learn from them. You might be surprised at the strength and growth you discover within yourself.

_____

_____

_____

_____

_____

_____

_____

How can you use what you learned from that tough day to help you in the present or future?

_____

_____

_____

_____

_____

_____

Remembering the lessons and growth from our past bad days can help us navigate future challenges with more resilience and positivity. By choosing to focus on the positive and seek out the lessons in our struggles, we can transform even the most challenging days into valuable experiences that help us learn, grow and thrive!

Change the way you look at things and
the things you look at change.

–Wayne Dyer

CHAPTER 9

FROM SETBACK TO SUCCESS

Simon Chan

FROM SETBACK TO SUCCESS
Simon Chan

I grew up as a shy, quiet Asian kid in Brooklyn, New York. The beginning of my path to becoming an entrepreneur can be traced back to a recommendation by a friend to read Robert Kiyosaki's book, *Rich Dad Poor Dad.*

At that time, I had a job I liked. It wasn't a high-paying job, but I enjoyed it. At the time, I thought I'd stay at the company forever and climb the corporate ladder. I didn't know about other options, like being an entrepreneur and not having to work at an office all day. Once I read *Rich Dad Poor Dad*, my eyes were open to the many possibilities, and I knew I needed to do something differently.

I wanted to have my own business where I could live a life of choice and freedom. I wanted to be free to choose where and when I worked. Even more importantly, I wanted to have passive income. Passive income is income that continues to pay you even when you're not working, such as rental property income or royalties or stock dividends.

I thought about starting a business franchise, but I didn't have the money to get started and a flexible lifestyle was important to me.

I continued to read books to find other ways I could own a business and make passive income. I read *Cashflow Quadrant* by Robert Kiyosaki and *Multiple Streams of Income* by Robert Allen. In reading these books, I learned I could earn passive income and create a flexible lifestyle with a home-based business.

I also read a book called *The Purpose Driven Life* by Rick Warren, and through that, came to discover my purpose is to have a positive impact on as many lives as possible.

I knew that whatever I did, it had to have God's blessing. I felt like starting a home business would allow me to help others too, and I always enjoyed helping people. Network marketing is not just about selling. It's really about impacting others if you want to create a long-term residual income.

When I started my first business in 2003, I set a goal to hit six figures of passive income within five years. I decided that if I didn't achieve this goal after five years, I would quit. However, if I quit before five years, I would be cheating myself because I knew that building a successful business requires consistent action over a significant period of time.

Being a devout Christian, I find Bruce Wilkinson's book *The Dream Giver* very insightful. It reminds me that God will never tempt me beyond what I can bear, and there's always a way out of difficult situations. Most people quit when faced with obstacles or setbacks instead of staying long enough to find that 1% or 10% improvement that will make a difference to help them forward. It could be a little tweak, a little change in habits or mindset or attitude that will determine success.

In my journey, I encountered one of my toughest moments back in 2004 after I went to my first network marketing company event, where I caught the vision to expand to Asia. I decided that when the company was ready to open in Asia, I was going to go there. Shortly after the company event, I heard rumors they were going to expand to Malaysia, and I decided to go—I wanted to be a pioneer. Now keep in mind my upline (the person who signed me up in my business), my mentor, had no experience growing into new markets, the company's products weren't approved, and they didn't have a business license to open there. I knew nothing about Malaysia at the time, but I was so excited! I was young, earning about $500 a month in my business, and I went there purely with determination.

I made several mistakes, including investing in an apartment and expanding to different cities too quickly. I also trusted the wrong people and almost got terminated from my company because I wasn't aware of the rules stating if you go too early and begin without the right license, you can get into big trouble. One of the very worst moments was trusting someone who was

NEVER QUIT ON A BAD DAY

going to be my future leader but who actually ended up betraying me and joining another team. So even though I'd built up a pretty good part-time business of $500 a month, I was about to lose it all because of my mistakes.

To continue to build, I had to beg forgiveness from compliance and change up my system and my presentations just to stay in the business. And thankfully, there were some people who stepped up to vouch for me. I promised to make changes.

At the same time, I was spending so much time in Malaysia that my United States-based business wasn't growing. In fact, it was shrinking. I was tempted to just throw in the towel in Malaysia and focus on the market in the United States. This was in October 2006. But I remembered one of the best pieces of advice I received, that the temptation to quit is greatest when success is right around the corner. So, I stayed.

Finally, in January 2007, the Malaysian market opened up, and I was able to grow my team of 400 people in just 30 days. It was the breakthrough I needed, and it eventually led me to the Philippines, where I built a team of over 80,000 people and helped build a six-figure residual income. I'm glad that I didn't quit on those bad days because the lessons I learned in the Malaysian market eventually created my explosive business growth in the Philippines.

So that's why I truly believe in never quitting on a bad day. Keep pushing even when things get tough. Remember that success is right around the corner, and you don't want to miss it by quitting too soon. Also, always have an exit strategy before entering anything. Having an exit strategy will help you stay focused on your long-term goals and keep yourself accountable. My initial exit strategy when I started my business was five years and obviously I did not quit after five years. It wasn't easy, but eventually I did hit my goal and built a seven-figure business.

When I reflect on my journey as an entrepreneur, I can't help but feel grateful for the tough times that almost made me quit. If I had given up during those moments, I would have never learned how to grow my business internationally. That experience eventually led me to expand to different countries, such as Thailand, Italy, Singapore, and Taiwan. None of that would have been possible if I had quit during those bad days.

Now, I know some of you might be thinking that you've never wanted to quit. But the harsh reality is that you haven't worked hard enough yet. If you haven't wanted to quit yet, it means you're not pushing yourself hard enough. You need to push yourself hard enough to reach a breaking point, because that's where success is. For every successful person, there have been breaking points, but they did not quit. And that's why they became successful.

One of the most important things I've learned from my mentor is to always end each activity on a positive note. For example, imagine it's the last ski run of the day. If you wipe out, fall and crash, then you may not be as excited to get back on the slopes the next day. If you end on a negative note, you're more likely to want to quit because it's harder to get started the next day.

My three boys love baseball and take it very seriously. I apply this same rule with them during our baseball practice, which we do seven days a week. We always end on a good hit, no matter how hard or easy it is. Because if they end on a bad hit, guess what they're thinking about? That bad hit, and they end up discouraged and don't want to practice the next day. Or they may even want to quit. The same principle applies to prospecting in your business. No matter what happens during the day, always end on a good note. It could be as simple as sending a follow-up text to a prospect, something simple like, "Hey, just checking in with you."

144

Always ending the day on a good note will encourage you to keep going and stay consistent.

Another reason I'm grateful for that string of bad days is it made me realize my lack of business experience and business maturity was the root cause. I often refer back to my late mentor's Jim Rohn quote, "Don't wish for fewer problems, wish for more wisdom."

And because I didn't quit, I've built a seven-figure MLM business and launched a second business focused on training people in the direct selling profession.

That advice I learned as a young entrepreneur really changed my life for the better and continues to inspire me. Understanding that keeps me focused. It motivates me to keep going, especially when times are tough. If you ever feel like quitting, just remember that success is right around the corner for you too!

ABOUT SIMON CHAN

Simon Chan is a Consistency Coach, speaker and author of the Amazon best seller, *The Consistency Pill: The 7 Step System to Increase Sales and Transform Your Business.*

He helps network marketers earn a part-time income of at least $1,000 a month by getting them to be consistent, defeat overwhelm and build a successful business online.

Simon is best known as the host of MLM Nation Podcast; the #1 network marketing podcast that features in-depth interviews with over 700 top income earners.

Simon started in network marketing in 2003 and built a million-dollar business with over 200,000 distributors by pioneering online duplication. He retired from building in 2013 to be a full-time trainer and founded MLM Nation.

Watch this video to hear Simon's heartfelt and encouraging message on growing through our challenging times!

SCAN THE QR CODE

REFLECTIONS ON RESILIENCE

It can be frustrating to stay focused on our goals when we aren't seeing the results as quickly as we'd like. Simon's favorite quote, "The temptation to quit is greatest when success is right around the corner," by Bob Parsons reminds us to keep going even when we are disappointed, as we are usually closer to a breakthrough than we think.

One of the success strategies Simon shared really resonates with me, and that is his tip on ending each activity and day on a positive note, which will keep us in the game a little longer. Simon's story reminded me of my time playing university soccer. Our coach had a similar approach to ending our practice sessions. Close to the end of each session, well before fitness activities, our coach would yell out, "next play." This signaled to us that the next outstanding play, whether it was a great shot, an impressive defensive stop, or even an excellent save, would be the end of practice for the day.

It was an incredible feeling when you and your teammates connected on a play, or you scored a remarkable goal, and that's how practice ended. This approach not only left us feeling accomplished and motivated, but it also reminded us of the importance of staying positive and striving for excellence in every moment.

What do you currently do to wind down at the end of the day? Do you typically do something to end your business/workday or evening on a positive note? It can be as simple as sending a message of appreciation to someone in your life.

Here are a few more examples of ways to end your workday or evening on a positive note:

- In business, take a few minutes to reach out and connect with a customer or team member or future customer or future team member.
- At work or home, take a few minutes to organize your desk and make an action item list for the next day. This will help you feel more in control and prepared to tackle whatever comes your way.
- Before bed, spend a few minutes doing a mindfulness exercise, breathing exercise, expressing gratitude or praying to help you relax and let go of any stress or tension from the day.

Starting today, what's one way you will end your workday or evening on a more positive note? Use one of the above examples or come up with your own. Write it in the space below.

_____

_____

Remember, small changes can have a big impact on our overall happiness and success. Let's take what we've learned from Simon's story and apply it to our daily lives to create more positivity and success.

You will never change your life until
you change something you do daily.
The secret of your success is found in
your daily routine.

–John C. Maxwell

CHAPTER 10

WHEN THE TIME IS RIGHT

Moving Forward for Success

WHEN THE TIME IS RIGHT
Moving Forward for Success

When you first heard the title of this book and while reading through the stories, you may have been thinking, "Phebe, are you saying I never can 'quit' something?" No, I'm not saying that at all. When you know a goal, a dream, a career, a relationship, a lifestyle choice, isn't serving you, your purpose or in alignment with your vision for your future then it may be time to make a change and move forward toward something else. What I am saying by "Never Quit on a Bad Day" is to make that decision on a "good day."

Why a good day? Because if you can transition away from something on a good day, then you are making the decision confidently without all the negative emotions that are typically associated with making a decision on a bad day. You are making that decision because you are looking at your future and realizing that where you are now and what you are doing isn't moving you closer to what you envision for yourself and your future.

WHEN I DECIDED IT WAS TIME TO RETIRE...

It was 2006 and I remember the day vividly when I decided to retire from the Vancouver Whitecaps soccer team. It was very early in pre-season and we had just finished an exhibition game. A new coach had taken over the team. We had a fabulous line up of talent and new players trying out for the upcoming season and we had played a great game. Personally, I was happy with my performance and knew I had played a good game. The new coach also had a lot of positive feedback for me after the game.

NEVER QUIT ON A BAD DAY

The season before we had finished 3rd in the W-League (the league we played in was called the W-League) and the year before that, we won the W-League Championship. I had so many incredible highs and challenging moments during my career with the Whitecaps.

I still remember my first session with the team like it was yesterday. I had played in Colorado the season before with the Fort Collins Force and as much as I enjoyed the experience, the club, my teammates, I decided that I wanted a chance to play with the incredible players back home who I spent so many years playing against as a youth player. At the time, the team was called the Vancouver Breakers, and the lineup was rock solid, so going into tryouts was nerve-wracking. I remember my excitement when the Coach told me he was signing me to the team, but getting signed was just the first step. Getting signed to a team doesn't necessarily mean playing time. From signing to dressing for games but sitting on the bench, to getting subbed in, to making the starting lineup, to contributing to the team' success, to being awarded W-League Player of the Year, it was a roller coaster of emotions but the one emotion that drove me forward was how much I loved to play soccer, how much I loved playing with my teammates, how much I loved playing in front of my friends and family and how much I loved to compete. I knew that retiring from the Whitecaps didn't mean I would stop any of that. I knew in my heart that I would

154

continue to play soccer, but I also knew that there were other areas of my life that were important to me, and it was time to focus on them.

As I drove home from the game, I was thinking of my future and other goals I had for my life, including my new life as an entrepreneur. As much as I loved playing, I knew that I had other goals that I wanted to accomplish. I pictured what life would look like not playing for the Whitecaps. What life would look like without the many hours of practices, games and time away on road trips. There were many family events that I had missed over the years, and I felt in my heart that it was time. I knew my priorities had shifted.

I took that evening to reflect on the decision that was in my heart. The decision was that it was time. The next day, I let the coach and the club know that I wouldn't be playing in the upcoming season. It wasn't after a bad game or bad practice that I made this decision. I made this decision, as I knew it was best for what I wanted my future to look like. I knew I would continue to play soccer and be involved in the sport (and yes, at the time of publishing this book, I do still play) but I knew that it was time for a shift and transition to focus on other areas of my life. I made that decision and felt a sense of peace mixed with excitement as to what was to come next.

Deciding when to quit or transition can be a challenging and a very tough choice, and there's no one-size-fits-all answer. Here are a few things you may want to consider when making a decision to transition to something new (and remember, make the decision on a good day):

1. If it's not aligned with your values: If what you're doing is in conflict with your personal values, it may be time to transition to something else.

2. If you have achieved what you set out to do: If you've accomplished your goals, it may be time to move onto something new.

3. If you are no longer growing or learning: If you feel like you're no longer developing new skills or knowledge, it may be time to move forward to new opportunities.

4. If you are not making progress despite your focused efforts: If you're putting in significant time and effort, but not seeing any progress or improvement, it may be time to consider a change.

5. If it is affecting your mental or physical health: If what you're doing is causing you significant stress, anxiety, or even physical health problems, it is worth considering whether it may be time to make a change. Be sure to evaluate whether this is just your comfort zone or if it is causing significant emotional anguish.

Transitioning to something new is deeply personal and will depend on your unique situation and future vision. Weighing the pros and cons on a good day and asking a trusted mentor or friend can be helpful too, but it's important to recognize the power of your own instincts and your intuition. Ultimately, it is up to you to determine the best path to creating a fulfilling future.

CHAPTER II

SUCCESS IS A JOURNEY

You've Got This!

SUCCESS IS A JOURNEY
You've Got This!

Throughout this book, you have read inspiring short stories about people, just like you, who have faced challenging times on their path to success. They faced obstacles, such as judgment, unexpected setbacks, financial hardships, and personal struggles, but they never gave up on their goals and dreams. Instead, they chose to believe in themselves and commit to their goals and dreams. Their stories, along with the exercises at the end of each chapter, have taught you that you, too, can overcome trials and achieve your goals.

By engaging in the Reflections on Resilience exercises in this book, you have tapped into your own inner strength. You have recognized the power of mindset and belief, how thoughts determine our actions, and learned how important it is to stay focused and positive in the face of obstacles.

As you continue on your own journey, it's essential to keep in mind that challenges and setbacks will come your way. Yet, the stories you've read have shown these obstacles and tough days are just part of the journey toward success. Instead of giving up on a bad day, approach tough times with courage and determination, and use challenging moments and days as opportunities to learn, grow, and develop new skills.

Remember that your success story is unique, and it will require patience, persistence, focus, and commitment. You must continue to believe in yourself, even in the face of adversity. Keep in mind that failure is not the opposite of success, but rather a stepping stone toward it. Learn from your setbacks, regroup, and keep moving forward.

By surrounding yourself with friends and a community who share your passion and vision, you will have a tribe of people who can support and cheer you on when times get tough. Find mentors who walked the path before you, and be open to learning from their experiences and insights.

I want to remind you that you have what it takes to overcome any obstacle and achieve greatness. You have the power within you to create the life you want and to fulfill your dreams. The journey may not be easy, but it will be worth it. Be intentional with your success and take action to do one thing every day that your future self will thank you for. You are capable of achieving amazing things, and the world is waiting for you and your story.

So, keep pushing forward, keep striving for greatness, and always remember...

AFTERWORD
by Vanessa Hunter

So, back to my question...

What makes some people persevere through the most monumental adversity while others crumble and quit at the slightest challenge? Having read these stories; I was struck by the common threads:

1. **Clarity** – When people have clarity of their purpose and goals, they are far less likely to quit. People who persevere often have a strong sense of what they are trying to accomplish and why it matters. This focus helps in the face of adversity.

2. **Determination** – When people are backed into a corner and feel they have no other options – they don't see quitting as an option either! Sometimes it's the lack of options or alternatives that helps them stay the course long enough to get through the obstacle.

3. **Resilience** – When people have a growth mindset, rather than a fixed mindset, they are more likely to consider something a setback rather than a failure. In other words, they see every challenge as an opportunity to learn and grow, therefore they are propelled forward and through the difficult times. They believe, as I do, that adversity teaches us lessons and lessons strengthen us.

4. **Strength** – When people are physically and emotionally strong, adversity doesn't seem so insurmountable. Making self-care and positive self-talk a habit now can prepare you for the inevitable challenges that will come your way later. The stronger you are going into it, the less likely you are to feel defeated because you'll have built up the endurance and mental fortitude of a champion.

5. **Support** – People who have supportive friends/ partners/peers find the strength to go on. We've all heard the saying; You are the average of the 5 people you hang out with. As you've read in some of these stories, sometimes we don't surround ourselves with the best cheerleaders. In fact, sometimes we align with people who sabotage their own lives and those of everyone around them. Keep your circle tight and trustworthy. Develop a strong support system before you actually need it by being strong for the people in your life and showing up for them as they face their own challenges.

6. **Faith** – People who believe that life will work out for them, that challenges happen FOR them, rather than TO them, and who operate with a sense of gratitude rather than attitude – are the ones who come out on top at the end of the day. And you know the saying; If they aren't on top, it's not the end!

And one final note:

Phebe Trotman, thank you for overcoming your fears and for being so clear on the purpose of this book. Thank you for being determined to serve people in a meaningful way. Thank you for your resilience throughout this process. Thank you for having the strength of a champion. Thank you for showing up and cheering people on. Thank you for keeping the faith!

Hi Friend,

You are an amazing and ambitious person who looks to make the most out of life, and I am thankful for who you are and the positive impact you will make on your community. The fact that you purchased this book and made it to this page shows your determination and drive. You have the potential and ability to turn your dreams into a beautiful reality.

I have been inspired by many individuals along my journey, and I wanted to create something that would encourage others as well.

Partial proceeds from all Never Quit on a Bad Day books and merchandise sales will go to Right to Play, as I believe sports/play is such a powerful vehicle for children to learn, grow, and develop, and to the Canadian Cancer Society. I lost my dad to cancer in 2012, causing some of the toughest days of my life.

Thank you for making a positive difference in the lives of others by being a part of and supporting the Never Quit on a Bad Day series.

Wishing you continued success,

KEEP YOUR COMMITMENT IN SIGHT

Are you focused on accomplishing a goal or big dream? Are you determined to push through your challenging days? Are you excited about your future?

Keep your commitment to your goals and dreams visible with a daily reminder.

Join the Never Quit on a
Bad Day Community

SCAN THE QR CODE

NEVER QUIT ON A BAD DAY™

A Guided Workbook for Creating Good Days

This workbook is designed to help you dream bigger dreams and create a life you love. By writing down your dreams and goals, you'll gain clarity, focus, and commitment. Studies have shown that writing down your aspirations can increase your likelihood of achieving them by up to 42%.

Never Quit on a Bad Day: A Guided Workbook for Creating Good Days includes insightful exercises, offering the freedom to express your thoughts, dreams, and goals. Let your dreams be your guiding light as you embrace the journey, and unleash your true potential!

Now Available on Amazon

SCAN THE QR CODE

Get Social & You May Be Featured as Our Never Quit on a Bad Day Enthusiast of the Month!

Inspire yourself and others to stay on track by sharing your Never Quit on a Bad Day commitment. Take a picture holding or wearing your 'Never Quit on a Bad Day' book, accessories, and/or clothing. Post the picture along with one of your goals on social media, and please tag us **@NeverQuitOnABadDay** and include the hashtag **#NeverQuitOnABadDay**. Every month, we will select one person to be featured on social media as our Never Quit on a Bad Day Enthusiast of the Month.

Together, let's create a ripple of positive change by encouraging others to commit to their goals and join Never Quit on a Bad Day community too!

LET'S CONNECT!

www.NeverQuitOnABadDay.com
IG: @NeverQuitOnABadDay
FB: NeverQuitOnABadDay

Sign up and join the Never Quit on a Bad Day community. Be the first to know about our next book release in the *Never Quit on a Bad Day* series, plus receive other insider perks too!

ABOUT PHEBE TROTMAN

Phebe Trotman is a successful and heart-centered entrepreneur based in Vancouver, Canada, who is passionate about helping others discover their joy. In both her athletic and professional careers, Phebe's personal success has been a testament that anything is possible with hard work, dedication, and a team-centered approach.

As an athlete, Phebe made a name for herself in the soccer world, achieving numerous awards and accolades. She has been inducted into the Coquitlam Sports Hall of Fame as an athlete, been honored as a team member in the BC Sports Hall of Fame and Museum, and recognized on two teams in the Burnaby Sports Hall of Fame. She is also listed on the BC Soccer Heritage Roll of Honour and holds several titles such as two-time Master's National Champion, W-League Champion, W-League Player of the Year, Women's Premier League National Champion, Simon Fraser University Female Athlete of the Year, NAIA Champion, NAIA Championship finals MVP, NAIA Women's Soccer Player of the Year, two-time First Team All-American, and Under-19 National Champion.

Phebe is committed to promoting the game of soccer. She is actively shaping its future through her coaching and mentorship of the next generation of players and coaches. Since 2009, Phebe has been leading the Coquitlam Metro-Ford Soccer Club Initiation Program for players aged three to seven years old. This program emphasizes skill development, physical literacy, and the improvement of psychomotor and cognitive skills, which prepare young players for success in the sport and in life.

In the business world, Phebe's drive and dedication propelled her to the top rank in her network marketing company. Phebe has received numerous company awards, including recognition as the Top International Customer Sponsor, Global Trainer of the Year, Runner Up Global Distributor of the Year, and Global Distributor of the Year. She has also been featured in magazines such as *Success From Home* and *Networking Times*, as well as on the #1 Global Podcast "MLM Nation" and in the book, *The Four Year Career for Women*.

Phebe is a champion for personal growth and believes that reaching one's full potential creates a ripple effect of inspiration and motivation. Phebe is passionate about helping others on their own journeys to unlocking their potential and living their best lives. With her dedication to empowering others, Phebe is a powerful force for positive change.

WITH HEARTFELT APPRECIATION

To my incredible *Never Quit on a Bad Day™ - Thriving Entrepreneurs* contributors: Jordan Adler, Jimmy Dick, Mike Dreher, Darren Ewert, Jen Furness, Jeanie Fountain, Steve Schulz, Dave and Roxanne Obiso, Scott Pospichal and Simon Chan. Thank you for saying yes! Without you and your inspiring example of persevering through tough times, this book would not have been possible. You have paved the way for others to follow, and your ability to overcome challenges with grace is truly remarkable. I thank you from the bottom of my heart for sharing your story. I look forward to what the future holds and am honored to have you as a friend and mentor. You have made a significant impact on my life, and I am forever grateful.

To my parents, Henderson and Joyce. Mom and Dad, your love and guidance have been the foundation of my life, and I am eternally thankful for the sacrifices you made to help me become the person I am today. Dad, although you may be in Heaven, I can hear you very (very) loudly cheering me on during the writing and release of this book. Thank you for always being my biggest champion. Mom, I'm so grateful for you. Your constant prayers, support and belief gives me the confidence to dream big and always pursue my life's passions.

To my brother TeRoi and Chanda. TeRoi, thanks for always inspiring me to be the best I can be in whatever I do in life; to take risks and to live a fun-filled adventurous life! Chanda, you are an incredible mother and I'm so thankful that I have a sister now too! I really appreciate all your support over the years. Skylar and Tatum, thanks for being the best nieces ever and helping me choose the background music for the book videos.

To the Trotman, Springer, Belgrave, Ewers, Ryan, Parsons, Watkins, Hunt, Lowe, Parkins, Sutherland, Branch, Clarke, Morrison, and Thunstrom families - you are simply the BEST! I am so thankful to have such a supportive and loving family who lead by example in caring for each other and loving others. Your support, love, and guidance have been key in helping me achieve my goals, and I feel blessed to have you all in my life.

Kori and Steven, thank you both for your continuous encouragement, support, mentorship, leadership, and prayers. Throughout our years of friendship, we have shared numerous exceptional experiences, and I believe we are just getting started. I am grateful for all the insight, wisdom, and love you have shown me. Sissy, your encouragement and guidance have been essential on my journey, and I am truly grateful for your presence in my life.

Vanessa, from the moment I shared the vision for this book series with you, you have been a constant source of encouragement. Your belief in me and the vision for this book series has been instrumental in making this first book a reality. Thank you for the beautiful foreword and afterword you wrote for this book. Your words set the perfect tone for the book. Thank you for your incredible friendship and mentorship throughout the years.

Virgil, thank you for being an incredible supporter throughout the process of writing this book. From the very first chat with you about my idea for this book, you have encouraged me and stood in my corner cheering for me. You have been by my side through every step, from the first look at book cover drafts, to the evolution of the logo, to the collection of stories and now, the finished book. Your love has been a true source of strength for me. Your belief in me and this book series has meant the world to me, and I am beyond grateful to have you in my life.

To my friends who are like family: Karlan, Ellice and Patrick, Sadie and Mark, Jenn, Jessie, Benny, Monique, Jameila, Sarah, Osita, Tanya, Shawndra, Renita, Natasha, Darron, Dowan, Modi, Danny, Kyla and Antonio, Duette, Casey, Michelle, KJ, Lisa, Ivan, Efe and Tom, you all are my tribe. I am truly blessed to have such outstanding people like you all in my life. Thanks for always keeping it real and being there through thick and thin. Your love and laughter over the years has lifted me up even during the hardest times of my life, and you always know how to make the good times even better. I cherish each and every one of you and feel incredibly grateful to have such an amazing group of friends in my life.

Kwame, thank you for the incredible impact you have had on my life. Your recommendation to read *Rich Dad Poor Dad* was a catalyst that set me on my entrepreneurial journey, and I am forever grateful for your guidance and encouragement over the years.

Mike and Darren, thank you for the extra gentle nudge (smile). It was through that impactful conversation that the seed for this book series was first planted.

Jordan, thank you for teaching me to write out my "perfect day". That one exercise and remembering my "perfect day" has been a lighthouse for me to focus on during life's challenging moments.

To my book designers, Margaret and Blake of Margaret Cogswell Designs, thank you for bringing my vision to life with your talent and creativity. Your ability to capture the essence of my message through your design has been truly remarkable. It has been a pleasure collaborating with you, and I want you to know how grateful I am to you for your dedication to this book series.

To my editor, Melody of Publishing Concierge, working with you on this project has been a lovely experience. From our very first conversation to the final moments of completing this book, your support and insightful feedback have been invaluable. Your guidance has been essential in shaping this book. I am grateful for you, your hard work and your incredible skill. This is just the beginning and I look forward to working with you on future books in this series.

To my proofreader, Julie of Creative Curvy Services, thank you for your attention to detail and suggestions as we worked together to create a polished final product.

To my brand strategist, Byron of Coastlines Creative Group, thank you for your hard work and dedication in creating an impressive logo to represent the essence of Never Quit on a Bad Day. I appreciate the time and research you put into this project.

To my website team, Sandro and Kelsey of Stigan Media, and Laura and the team at Virtual Squirrel Business Support Services, your skills and expertises have helped me to create a beautiful and professional online presence. Your creativity and passion shine through in all that you do.

To my wonderful team of Advanced Readers Copy (ARC) readers, Michelle, Renne, Terry, Ivan, John, Renita, Sarah, Duette, Efe, and Liam, thank you for saying yes and your willingness to help. I asked each of you because of the tremendous respect I have for you and your support over the years. I appreciate your feedback and I am grateful to have you on my ARC team and more importantly, in my life.

Kody B. and Jodi, thank you for creating a phenomenal movement that I'm honored to be associated with. Over the years, I have learned so much from both of you. You have taught me the immense power of acting on promptings and how we can change not only our own life but the lives of others as well. KB, I am especially grateful to you for planting the seed many years ago that inspired me to share this story. As you always say, "The story in your mind becomes the story of your life" and here we are.

Team Legacy and Team Impact, you are all simply amazing! As I think of all the team members, past and present, who have said 'yes', my heart fills with gratitude. Your dedication and passion for pursuing your dreams are truly inspiring. We have shared so many fantastic moments and watching you all achieve great things in your lives fuels my own determination to keep pushing forward. I love seeing you all shining in your own unique ways, and I want you to know that I will always be your biggest cheerleader, rooting for you in everything you do.

Dave O., thank you for knowing that SOC was for me before I knew it was for me.

To the fabulous SOC Corporate Executive Team, SOC Customer Success Team: Walter, Sandra, Kathy, Jen, John and team, my fellow Eagles: Jordan, Bob and BettyAnn, Diane, Melissa and the incredible SOC field leaders: Dave and Lori, Callie, Gayle and Steve, Judy, Willie, Shawn, Joy, April, Dhea, and the SOC affiliates - past and present, you are a group of truly exceptional people. I'm continually inspired by you and your dedication to positively changing lives with the message of promptings. I have learned so much from you all over the years. You all have such big hearts and I'm honored to be a part of such a supportive and uplifting community. Thank you for being a part of this journey with me.

To the CMFSC Technical Team: Sara, Alfredo, Andrea, Liam, Lindsay, Michelle, Esteban and Dale; Alex and the CMFSC Board; Rae; Neil and Initiation Program Staff Coaches, I feel incredibly fortunate to be part of a coaching crew that is so dedicated and passionate about soccer. Your enthusiasm and commitment to helping young players develop and grow both on and off the field is truly inspiring. I have learned so much from each of you, and it is an honor to work alongside such talented and dedicated coaches.

To Ps. Durwin; Ps. Troy and Rachel; Ps. Shane and Rachel (and the Resonate family), your unwavering faith has been a constant source of inspiration, and thank you for reaching out to connect at times when I've always needed it the most.

To Cory, Erin and my Coquitlam FBBC Family, thank you for pushing me to my limits and inspiring me to be the best version of myself. Your dedication to health and wellness has been a constant reminder of the importance of taking care of ourselves both physically and mentally.

To my BNI Marinaside Family, I feel like I've grown up in business with you all. I'll be forever grateful for the impact you have had on me personally and professionally. I could not have made it this far as an entrepreneur without your support and guidance.

To my soccer teammates, past and present, as I look back on my many years of playing soccer, my heart is filled with appreciation as I remember all the incredible lifelong friendships I have made through this sport. From the celebrations and laughter to the heartbreak and even tears, we have shared so many moments together. I want to express my deep gratitude for always inspiring me to work hard both on and off the field. Your commitment to working hard and achieving our goals as a team has taught me valuable lessons about teamwork and dedication. I am grateful for the many lessons I have learned from each and every one of you over the years.

To my soccer coaches, throughout my life, I have been fortunate to have had many coaches who have taught me invaluable lessons about leadership, inspiration, and teamwork. From my childhood to now, each coach has imparted their unique wisdom, helping me to better understand how to motivate and unite a team to work towards a shared goal. I am grateful for the lessons I have learned from each of you, as these have helped shape me into the leader I am today. Thank you for all that you have taught me over the years, and for instilling in me the values of hard work, integrity, and dedication.

To you, the reader, again I want to express my sincerest gratitude for taking the time to read this book. I pray that the stories and insights shared throughout, along with the Reflections on Resilience exercises, have provided you with the empowerment and encouragement needed to persevere through tough times. **Remember, success is within your reach, and Never Quit on a Bad Day!**

WORDS OF PRAISE
What Readers Are Saying

Must Read!

Loved how this book was set up with easy to read stories and reflection exercises that can be read cover to cover or modularly. Each testimony was well captured; personal with purpose. As someone who can lack the time and focus to read, I found these burst of inspiration just what I needed! Thank you Phebe!! Looking forward to the series to come.

-Lynn

Such profound Encouragement!

While reading the Never Quit on a Bad Day stories and watching the videos of these accomplished entrepreneurs/business builders, it was refreshing to learn about the underbelly struggles, victories, and fulfillment that each transparently revealed. I felt reminded and encouraged throughout my own success journey. The reflection pages are heartwarming and reawakening for the soul. This quick read will serve as a support system in your life's continuous success story.

-Amazon Customer

A MUST READ! WHAT PERFECT TIMING!

I am so grateful I grabbed this book! As an Entrepreneur in the Network Marketing space, it is so easy to get down on ourselves when we judge or define our success on our volume, or merely numbers. One of the biggest gifts from this book is that it reminded me how important building community is, and without a Tribe of truly aligned connections, it is a difficult task to continue to have the driving force to Succeed.

This read came to me at the perfect time to remind myself what I need to focus on to continue to shine my gifts with the World. It also reminded me that we are never alone. We can depend and count on people to stand beside us and remind us of our worth, when we may sometimes forget.

A MUST READ for any Entrepreneur or anyone for that mater that is wanting to grow and make a difference!

-Diane Lauzon

A must read for all dreamers.

Never Quit on a Bad Day is an uplifting look at how to conquer the obstacles that stand in the way of your ultimate goal. I loved that it didn't just make me think about my own goals but how I support those around me and what role am I playing to them. Each story is short but impactful with a beautiful and easy to connect with message (even though I've never flown a helicopter). This book will undoubtedly have a positive impact on your life and those around you.

-Amazon Customer

Must Read for ALL Aspiring Successful Entrepreneurs

Everyone with big dreams and desires to succeed will benefit by the stories within the book. It's important for any of us 'go getters' to recognize and embrace the common obstacles that present along the way to our successes. This read is valuable with all the added tools and exercises we can do, that help up embrace the journey and build our resilience. IMO Excellent content. Come see for yourself.

-Teresa Brown

We would LOVE to hear from you!

Please take a moment to share your thoughts in an honest review, as your feedback is greatly appreciated.

www.NeverQuitOnABadDay.com/Review

Made in the USA
Middletown, DE
14 October 2023

40801574R00104